A HUMBLE
*C*ONFIDENCE

A Humble Confidence

A Christian Perspective on Self-Image

Dave Ames

MISSION TO MARRIAGE

Mildenhall

Bible quotations (unless otherwise stated)
are from the New International Version

© International Bible Society 1973, 1978, 1984

Cover design by **Steve Ayres**

Cartoons reprinted by permission of
Word Publishing

Editor: Nina Rye

British Library Cataloguing in Publication Data Ames, Dave
A Humble Confidence.
1. Psychology - Christian perspective
ISBN 1-898859-01-9
Printed in Great Britain for
MISSION TO MARRIAGE
20 Mill Street, Mildenhall, Suffolk IP28 7DP

by

Indeprint
99 Marlow Road, London SE20 7XW

Dedication

This book is dedicated to our children Michael, Patricia and Billy, who reached adulthood about the time I was mature enough to have any hope of being a successful parent. The fact that they have turned out to be the kind of people with which Joyce and I are proud to be associated is the grace of God.

Acknowledgements

'Wounds from a friend can be trusted.' (Proverbs 27:6). Criticism, like some dear friends, isn't always comfortable to live with, but in the end it can prove to be the most profitable friend. I have benefited even from criticism that was never intended to be friendly and from having my ears pinned back in polemical discussions with men like Jay Adams and others less renowned. All of it helped me to identify many of the triggers that erect barriers in the minds of others precluding them from effectivly interacting with new ideas.

However, I also find it necessary to have people who are willing to think with me and still be critical enough to ensure things are worded in the most precise way possible. I want to thank particularly Vina Green, Geraldine Booker and our hard working editor Nina Rye for taking the trouble to provide this necessary service. It may be possible to write a helpful book without such help, but I hope I never have to do so.

CONTENTS

Foreword
by Selwyn Hughes

Self-image is in the news! No subject seems to be of more importance to the contemporary Christian Church, yet no subject is more prone to confusion. Psychological theories concerning this issue abound and mixed with a selective use of Scripture, are sometimes used to perpetuate false ideas and produce unhealthy believers.

With wonderful good sense, Dave Ames cuts through much of today's confusion on the subject of self-image and brings us back to a clear Biblical understanding of the issue. I have long admired the author's knack at getting to the heart of issues, his ability to think clearly, his eagerness to pursue truth, but what I admire above all is his firm and unswerving commitment to Scripture.

The Bible after all is the only true guide in helping us understand the essential nature of human existence. I am constantly appalled however at how many modern day writers misuse and misapply the Scriptures when writing on the subject of self-image. This book is different. The author's careful treatment of the well known but often misunderstood text: 'love your neighbour as yourself', is just one example of his understanding and faithfulness to Scripture.

One would think that becoming a Christian would eliminate any problem of self-image. After all, the gift of Jesus Christ and eternal life gives us something far more important to think about than ourselves. Once we become sons and daughters of God how can we possibly question our basic worth? Nevertheless Christians do struggle over this issue and in consequence yield to deep discouragement and fear. Many live out their days with what can only be described as a weak or bad self-image.

A major reason for this is a common misunderstanding about the nature of humility. Bernard of Clairvaux, when asked to name the four most cardinal virtues replied: 'Humility! Humility! Humility! Humility!' But a lot that is taught in the Christian Church about humility is really nothing more than self belittlement in disguise. It is only when we understand what humility is and comprehend its true characteristics, that we will be able to act with that 'humble confidence' - which is the title and thesis of this monograph.

I think you are going to enjoy your time spent in the pages of this book. When I first perused it I had the image of a doctor walking into a stuffy and closed-up room of one of his patients and throwing open the windows to let in a stream of much needed fresh air. The 'fresh air' in this case is the pure oxygen of the Scriptures. But now let me step aside and let you enjoy the experience for yourself.

Introduction

I am dyslexic. When I entered school my whole world of achievement centred around the very things that dyslexics cannot seem to do. Like all dyslexic children I was a poor reader and a terrible speller. Unfortunately, I began elementary school light years before this phenomenon had been discovered. Once someone got the idea that I was not retarded, they were sure I was just plain lazy. Neither label, 'retarded' nor 'lazy', is a particularly good ingredient for a healthy self-image.

I also grew very fast (I was 6 feet tall at the age of 12) which added two complications. First, I was not just a dumb kid, I was a big dumb kid. Secondly, my co-ordination was a long time in coming.[1] Consequently, another great portion of my life was blighted. Most non-academics can look back on their early school years and at least state that they excelled in playground activities. I could not. I was always at the losing end of the inevitable playground fights. If I ever won, it was never a credit to me because I was so much bigger than the little wiry opponent who started the fight to boost his social status. My name may have been David but I was always cast in the role of Goliath.

Being awkward at sports presents a problem to any male youth, but the problem is doubled when you are the biggest kid in the school and don't even have an academic reputation to fall back on. Take the great American game of baseball for instance, where I was good at everything except throwing, catching and batting. In my first year on the basketball team I only scored two points all year in spite of the fact that I was a foot taller than almost every kid in the league. As I look back I can't see how I stuck it out. I must have been desperate.

My mother, who was not terribly secure herself, was very disappointed in my school performance and she showed it. My sports-minded uncles and grandfather were disappointed in my lack of co-ordination and they couldn't seem to conceal their disappointment either. It would seem that I had no redeeming feature to endear me to anyone important in my life: the kids at school, my parents or even my extended family. Not the optimal ground work for readily reaching my potential. I know that I am certainly not unique as a late bloomer, and it is only in Christ - and understanding his plan for my life - that I have even begun to blossom at all. Back in my teens I simply concluded that I was not worth very much.

I am quite sure my situation is repeated a million times over. People are presented with certain skills, abilities and attributes which are promoted as the currency of a society and according to this standard they require supplementary benefits to survive. The society we live in teaches its standards all too well.

In the eyes of secular man, the meaning and purpose of life lies in such things as possessions, prestige, position or power: we are what we own, what we look like or what we can do. Advertisers reinforce this message every day, and make their living from it. It follows that the measure of a man rests in his ability to obtain the right commodities.

Christians, on the other hand, do not accept such materialistic standards. God has let us know that the meaning and purpose of life lies in a quite different direction. Therefore, the basis of our self-image is also quite different.

1. I have recently been told that poor co-ordination is another symptom of dyslexia.

Chapter 1

A HUMBLE CONFIDENCE

We have it on the authority of Genesis 2:7 that man was constituted of the dust of the earth and the breath of God. It follows then that without God we are nothing but dust. Jesus will never leave us or forsake us, but when we allow sin to separate us from his fellowship we definitely feel like dust. Self-image problems frequently involve considerations other than our own sin, but the antidote for all of them involves a right relationship with God.

The term 'a humble confidence' is meant to convey something of the dynamic of a Christian self-image. The words confidence and humility, might appear to be opposites; a 'humble confidence' might sound like a paradox. But I don't believe God sees it that way. When we think of the Lord Jesus, most of us imagine a confident person who knew exactly what he intended to accomplish and what it was going to cost. At the same time we know he was 'gentle and humble in heart'.[1]

In speaking to those who have had their lives dramatically changed through their relationship with Jesus, these two qualities, humility and confidence, seem almost invariably to be in evidence. Testimonies frequently reveal a pattern: losers find purpose in Christ and become winners. Even those who seem to be winning but in reality have no meaning or purpose, find Christ and become winners in the really important things of life. It may be called the baptism in the Holy Spirit, the filling of the Spirit, or coming under the Lordship of Christ, the fact is that someone who was only marginally committed is now totally committed to all that God wants to do in his or her life. Occasionally it's a new convert who takes God seriously right from the start, which is exactly the way he intended all along.

Volumes have been written to describe the crucial events or required steps leading to this experience, but the essence is that the person turns over every bit of their life and God takes control. As Ian Thomas would put it: 'I vacate and the Lord Jesus occupies'. However, when it comes to describing the results in plain English, it is difficult to avoid the fact that this person's new perspective on God has given them a new outlook on themselves - a new self-image.

This is not because acquiring a new self-image is presented as an expectation. Nor is it due to a renewed interest in self, quite the opposite is actually true; those who are really under the control of the Spirit become much more concerned with others and less with them-

15

selves. A part of the reason why these people, now rightly related to God, are far less taken up with themselves is that they view themselves from an entirely different perspective. Therefore, I think it fair to conclude that when Jesus Christ becomes the dominating force in an individual's life, there is a change in self-image.

For some this idea poses problems: being Spirit-filled (and all the various terminology involved) is theological, but self-image is considered to be psychological. Men like Jay Adams, Paul Brownback, Paul Vitz[2] and a host of others have written at length of the pitfalls of the present obsession with self and self-image. Their books show how much secular humanism has been piggy-backed into the church through indiscriminate borrowing from secular psychology. This has been a great and valuable ministry - someone needs to keep us alert. If nothing else, they have made all who would address this subject (including myself) much more aware of the problems.

However, being alert to areas where secular psychology contradicts Christian doctrine is cold comfort to those feeling totally inadequate. The position is sometimes taken that the Bible doesn't teach on self-image and, therefore, we have no mandate to do so either. After all, if this is really a by-product of being baptised in the Spirit then surely we just simply need to be encouraging such people to 'get right with God'. This is exactly what needs to happen, but such a statement isn't sufficiently specific to provide 'handholds' on the problem.

There are plenty of committed, Spirit-filled Christians around the world with problems they really shouldn't have, when they actually possess the Holy Spirit and the entire shopping list of spiritual fruit listed in Galatians chapter 5. It is because we do have problems holding onto our inheritance in various areas that God provided some to minister in teaching, preaching, counselling, prophecy and various other gifts. As with any other life problem, the Word has answers and they are not the vague euphemisms which are all too often thrown about so lightly. There are some very specific nuts-and-bolts solutions, or handholds.

I wholeheartedly agree with Messrs. Adams, Brownback and Vitz that modern psychology is not the place to look for answers to self-image problems. One of psychology's major objectives is for us to be comfortable with ourselves, but the only self that psychology is aware of is our old nature. One of God's primary objectives is that we become comfortable walking in our new nature. The distinction between the Christian and secular approaches to self-image will become even more obvious as we progress.

DEFINITIONS

Before we go any further we need to define some terms and develop some strategy for our investigation. It has been said that humans alone of all God's earthly creation have self-awareness. Whether that is true or not, we can't avoid the fact that all humans have self-awareness and that it seems to be the source of a lot of heartache. There isn't a term involving this self-awareness that hasn't been used extensively by psychologists. We can't, however, afford to surrender all descriptive terms to those who happen to popularize them. Psychology doesn't own such terms as self-image or self-esteem any more than sex is the private domain of Playboy magazine.

First a definition of terms:

> Self-image is simply the way I see myself.
> Self-consciousness is a concern with how others see and value me.[3]
> Self-centredness is viewing every life experience as to how it affects me, in the extremity, oblivious to others.
> Selfishness is wanting things my own way, in the extremity, regardless of the cost to others.

The Oxford dictionary defines self-image as 'one's idea of what one is'. The term is not found in the Bible, but then neither is 'the Trinity'. The Bible undoubtedly has a lot to say on the Trinity but it also has a terrific amount to say on self-image, an idea we will begin unpacking in the next chapter. There is certainly more specific biblical terminology dealing with self-image than the Trinity.

It is reasonable to expect that one must understand humanity before developing an approach to human problems. But for a truly Christian strategy, this basic sequence must be followed:

1. Understand God;
2. Understand man;
3. Develop a strategy for tackling a human
   problem.

The priority of perception is understanding God in order
to comprehend man in order to deal with a human
problem. Or to use more academic terms, theology,
anthropology, then methodology. Unfortunately, it is
not always possible to divide all the information into
three neat categories and still put forth a readable
declaration, because they spill over into each other. But
it helps to keep this order in mind, in sifting through all
the available data on this topic of self-image.

DEFINING THE PROBLEM

Now that we have defined terms and the direction we
want to take, we need to define the problem. In keeping
with our other definitions, a self-image problem would
be an inaccurate view of oneself. This could involve
pride, inferiority or even a lateral inaccuracy, a person
with one gift perceiving themselves as possessing another,
just not finding their niche. Realistically speaking, the
most common problem is people who are, to some
degree, crippled by feelings of inferiority, and therefore
that will be our major concern.

The next consideration: What caused this inaccurate
self-image that is crippling us? There is little doubt that
parents, teachers and peers all contributed to the way we

view ourselves, and their input definitely cannot be ignored. We also can't ignore the fact that while children are good observers, they are not so good at interpretation, and some of the hurt and rejection stored away are simple misunderstandings. However, a substandard childhood is not the real core of the problem: quite a number of people have had extremely deprived childhoods and yet still have bags of confidence. Whose fault is it that I have a poor self-image? Is it my parents' [and the others'] fault, or do I bear some of the responsibility? Most of us would tend to fix the blame on those individuals and situations that we believe robbed us of self-worth. The issue of responsibility may seem unnecessary and even dangerous. After all, what will it do for my already sagging self-image if I have to assume even a small part of the responsibility for it?

Identifying responsibility can bring guilt or it can bring hope. If I identify where I have gone wrong, then the chances are I can correct it and avoid making the same mistake in the future. There can be no such hope in blaming others.

It is not so much a question of fixing blame as determining what we can do to become survivors. Do icy roads cause accidents, or does the way we drive on icy roads cause accidents? Do all people who drive on icy roads have accidents? Of course not! In fact most of them don't. Those who survive slow down, maintain a good distance between themselves and the car ahead, and so on.

The fact is that most of us have to learn to survive a less than optimal childhood. Both my wife Joyce and I frequently ask seminar groups for a show of hands of those who have had a really good childhood; it is generally less than 25 percent who raise their hands. I often suspect that many who do raise their hands do so out of loyalty to their parents, which is a good attitude, but they still had to make a fair effort to survive. I say this because occasionally I see people raise their hands whom I know didn't have much of a childhood.[4]

The biblical approach to the problem would centre more around where we base our self-image than the hazards we have had to survive.

The above statement means we are actually discussing rightly- or wrongly-based self-images, which is why I find the term self-image the most convenient. An image is very neutral, allowing discussion on such things as accuracy or inaccuracy and right or wrong self-images. Esteem, on the other hand, is a sort of 'tram line' value, with high self-esteem at one end and low at the other. It is therefore limited and can be misleading. There is also a connotation problem with the term self-esteem in a Christian context. It may well be that esteem is used simply as regard, but the thesaurus in my word processor offers up such synonyms and associations as honour, revere, admiration and even worship. Most Christians would have greater difficulty discussing self-admiration than they would sex.

Christians are the only ones with a hope of a rightly based self-image, but we have an additional obstacle to obscure the truth - the misuse of Scripture. Christians will always be confused on the issue of self-image if we believe we should magnanimously give of ourselves to others, while at the same time, believing ourselves to be worthless, for the simple reason that it is a contradictory message. The Bible definitely won't support the oft quoted axiom 'You can't love others until you love yourself'.[5] At the same time love is giving, and if we believe we are worthless we don't believe we can give anything of value. If Christians are going to be givers, we need an identity that helps us discern what we have to give. Otherwise, it becomes all too easy to view love simply as a means of having our own needs met rather than giving to the needs of others.

Our Christian minds automatically counter terms like 'feelings of insecurity' with 'security in Christ'. But it's not as straightforward as our knee-jerk reaction might imply; there are complications. Security comes through relationship with Christ and yet the relationships he calls us into are the very conditions that reveal our insecurity. Insecurity is entirely relative to those with whom we are attempting to relate: 'Why would they want to know me?' Trust is the functional core of relationships, which makes trust the exact point where insecurity spoils things. This even extends to our relationship with God: 'Why would he want to know me?' Many insecure people don't believe God really loves them. They won't trust God to be true to his word.

Insecurity is a disproportionate sense of vulnerability. We feel sure we will be rejected in some way. Before a relationship can be really operative we must trust the other party to carry out their responsibility. This is true whether it is a co-operative relationship where two people join together to accomplish a given task, or a social relationship which is an end in itself. Trusting someone requires that we make ourselves vulnerable - in peril of being let down. Real trust means we make ourselves so vulnerable that we don't have any emergency plans. However, the more we've been hurt the less willing we are to make ourselves vulnerable and we find trust virtually impossible. We say we are trusting even though we may have very dependable contingency plans. Even with God, we say we are trusting and still have very dependable contingency plans just in case we are disappointed.

Such general facts as 'God is love' and 'He will never leave us or forsake us', form a protective umbrella until certain specific questions usher in sufficient doubt to make it seem as if the umbrella is ten feet above our heads in a driving rain. 'If God is really looking out for you, why didn't he let you score just one more point to pass your qualifying exams, after all the work you put in?' The basic proposition is no less valid but it seems so because our faith in God has been 'embarrassed' by a question that casts doubt on his integrity or ability. Questions like: 'Why does God allow suffering?', are usually designed to imply that our faith is not relevant to 'the real world', and subtly, that is exactly what it is causing us to believe, that Christianity is irrelevant to our everyday life.

Throughout this book we will be examining the issues behind the questions that seem to poke holes in our umbrella, such as:

To what extent is our self-image pre-programmed by our childhood experiences, and just how indelible is such early childhood programming?

What is the effect of our current successes or failures?

Can we actually survive without some 'positive strokes'?

Is it possible to love others if we don't love ourselves?

Is self-love biblical?

Should we view ourselves as worms?

How can we read the Bible's picture of the total depravity of the human race and not feel like a worm?

Are we supposed to feel good about ourselves? Is it unhealthy not to?

How is it possible to feel good about ourselves even when actual performance figures seem to prove we are inferior?

Is it possible even though we know we are dealing with a sin problem?

How can we even lift up our heads when we know our real identity is that of an impossible wretch?

How do I remove barriers that prevent my development to a healthy self-image?

1. Matthew 11:29
2. Jay E Adams, <u>The Biblical View of Self-Esteem, Self-Love, Self-Image</u> (Harvest House); Paul Brownback, <u>The Danger of Self-Love</u> (Moody Press); Paul Vitz, <u>Psychology as Religion - The Cult of Self-Worship</u> (Lyon). All very worthwhile reading.
3. Self-consciousness could also be simply being conscious of oneself or self-awareness.
4. I knew about their childhood through counselling them.
5. None of the commands to love neighbour, one another, spouse or enemy has any exception for those who haven't had their needs met by the significant others in their lives and therefore don't feel good about themselves. I recognize that reaching out in love is easier for a secure person than for one who is insecure, but the Bible seems to take the trust and obey tack knowing the resources are provided by God.

Chapter 2

HUMILITY

We have established at least a sketchy definition of the problem. We also know that we need to look to God to understand man before we can begin developing a strategy. However, looking to God for a human self-image model could sound a bit impractical, considering the number of people in mental institutions who believe they are God.

There is also the seeming irrelevance of fallen man looking at a perfect God. What is God's self-image? Among other things he must see himself as perfect, which is certainly no help to me. How did Jesus see himself? Philippians 2:6 tells that Jesus saw himself as equal to the Father. However, that would seem to be more in regard to his position in the God Head. There is a reference to Jesus' self-image in the gospel of John that would seem to be more closely linked with his humanity: 'Jesus knew that the Father had put all things under his power, and that he had come from God and was returning to God'. But the next two verses demonstrate a slightly different dimension: 'So he got up from the meal, took off his outer clothing, and wrapped a towel around his waist. After that, he poured water into a basin and began to wash his disciples' feet, drying them with the towel that was wrapped around him'.[1]

MEEKNESS AND MAJESTY

It is not coincidental that Scripture places this very rare statement of Jesus' self-awareness along side his volunteering to do one of the most servile acts known in that culture. Not only does it link authority with servanthood, it also takes human worth and identity out of the realm of mortal prominence and connects it firmly to God. Jesus placed himself in a pretty vulnerable position by doing this, but he could afford to do so because his security didn't come from his role as Rabbi, Master or leader of his disciples but from his Father.

As mentioned in the opening chapter, Jesus was humble, and that does have relevance. One Christian leader recently wrote, 'I have always thought it interesting that people who are the farthest from the Lord are those who are impressed with their own goodness, while those who are closest to him seem to be more conscious of their own sin....Is it because the white light of God's holiness acts like an X-ray that enables people to see more clearly what is going on in the core of their beings?'[2] Isaiah got close to God and said, 'Woe is me.. I am ruined! For I am a man of unclean lips.'[3] Hardly the type of statement one would expect from a positive self-image. How could Paul say, 'Nothing good lives in me' and have a healthy self-image?

Both Isaiah and Paul came to grips with their own personal worthlessness in the presence of the holiness of God, but they didn't base their self-image on it. Nor did

27

they kid themselves that their rottenness was just a bad dream: they faced it squarely, and then encountered the grace of God. As the patriarch of revival through repentance, Roy Hession loved to say, 'To qualify for God's grace we have only to admit we need it'. Isaiah and Paul came face to face with God, knew they needed his grace and weren't afraid to admit it. So much for self-image one might say. But the moment they admitted their need they were cleansed.

God ordered one of the seraphs to take a live coal from the altar and cleanse Isaiah's lips. Then, something even more remarkable, this man who had just admitted to having unclean lips is offered the position of ambassador. The first words out of God's mouth were, 'Whom shall I send? And who will go for us?' Isaiah's reply: 'Hear am I. Send me'[4]; and God accepted. What else could give a greater boost to his sense of significance?

Paul's Damascus Road experience, although different, has striking similarities, particularly the immediate offer to join God's team. We also get some very useful insights into his thoughts about himself as he functioned on that team. There is a paradoxical balance between the awareness of one's rottenness through experiencing the holiness of God and being his 'chosen instrument'.[5]

We can conclude from these examples that weakness doesn't prevent greatness in God's economy. Once we accept this we are much less reluctant to acknowledge our weaknesses and confess our sins. This in turn means that God doesn't have to devote as much of our time together working on us and can now begin working through us. Isaiah and Paul didn't become great men of God until they freely admitted how really 'ungreat' they were.

The biblical term for a rightly based self-image is humility.

Humility is: functioning in the awareness that anything of eternal significance, happening in or through my life, is of God. I can't take credit for it.

The reason that self-image appears in the subtitle to this book and not humility, is because the connotation of the word humility has so shifted that most people understand humility more as self-effacement than anything associated with a healthy self-image.

WORDS WITH BAGGAGE

Dictionary definitions of humble/humility range from healthy terms like *unassuming* and *unpretentious* to sickly words such as *inferior*, *shameful*, *crushed* and *worthless*. Humility is actually seen as the reverse of a healthy self-image. I don't think this has as much to do with us being the prideful creatures we are as with word association. Most dictionaries and even the Bible, use humility as an antonym to pride which is an attitude of superiority. It is easy to assume from such a model that humility has the same association with inferiority that pride has with superiority. This is a common error in logic. It assumes right and wrong are always at opposite extremes failing to comprehend that often both extremes are wrong. Humility is as far removed from inferiority as it is from superiority (see figure 1). From any point of the triangle the other two points are extreme. Humility differs from both superiority and inferiority in that they are relative terms, while humility is not.

Humility

Pride (superiority)   Inferiority

Figure 1.

Observing the life of the Lord Jesus it is obvious that inferiority has nothing to do with humility. One would not associate inferiority with Jesus, and yet he could say 'By myself I can do nothing; I judge only as I hear, and my judgment is just, for I seek not to please myself but him who sent me'.[6] This passage confirming the dependency of Jesus on the Father is not an isolated text, it is a major theme throughout the gospel of John. It also verifies our definition of humility: 'The understanding that anything of eternal significance, happening in or through my life, is of God'.

The fact that I feel it necessary to use the term self-image, because of the connotations of grandeur in the word esteem, might be seen as a foible, but it is a harmless foible compared to losing the richness of the word humility due to popular implications. It isn't too great a problem to have to scrape around to find a new term to replace an old man made term, but we run into problems when we lose the value of biblical terminology. I am not an advocate of Christian jargon or of limiting our vocabulary to biblical terms, but I am on guard against key biblical concepts being blurred by social evolution.

We are told that Moses was a very humble man, more humble than anyone else on the face of the earth.[7] However, he wasn't displaying it when he swaggered down among his people hoping to exhibit his leadership skills by killing the Egyptian. Neither was he demonstrating humility when he gave God all those excuses at the burning bush.

'What if they do not believe me?'[8]

'I am slow of speech and tongue.'[9]

'Why would Pharaoh listen to me?'[10]

'O Lord, please send someone else to do it.'[11]

These were manifestations of inferiority and not humility.

Considering the Lord's statement, 'By myself I can do nothing' quoted earlier, I think it is a fair assumption that Moses ultimately entered his 'historically documented' state of humility when he finally and firmly understood what was required of him. Moses eventually realised that neither the fact that he had been 'educated in all the wisdom of the Egyptians',[12] nor that he had hidden away on the back side of a mountain for forty years, had any bearing on his ability to do what God was asking. All God wanted was for Moses to be available and God would do the rest. Possibly the penny finally dropped when God said, 'See, I have made you like God to Pharaoh, and your brother Aaron will be your prophet'.[13]

HUMILITY REQUIRES
SELF-ASSESSMENT

Humility is definitely self-oriented terminology. The state of being either humble or proud implies self-assessment. If I speak of someone else's humility or pride I am usually making assumptions about their self-assessment. The Bible does link humility with concern for others: 'With humility of mind let each of you regard one another as more important than himself',[14] but it is still relative to self. A self-focus does not necessarily have to involve self-centredness, it may be a self-inventory or an attempt to orient oneself: 'How do I fit into the scheme of things?' A godly self-focus is meant to lead us to the conclusion: 'By myself I can do nothing'.

It is this godly self-inventory that brings the understanding of which James speaks: 'Who is wise and understanding among you? Let him show it by his good life, by deeds done in the humility that comes from wisdom'.[15] Wisdom and understanding are from the Lord, but they are to be grasped with the intellect; they are of the mind and not the emotion. This is important because self-image problems are almost always driven by the emotions rather than the mind. So we begin with 'the understanding that anything of eternal significance, happening in or through my life, is of God'.

GOD OPPOSES THE PROUD

Then we can move on to understand some of the resources available to make these eternally significant things happen. There is an extremely noteworthy statement which appears three times in the Bible, 'God opposes the proud but gives grace to the humble'.[16]

There is a lot in this declaration. The proud are those who do not acknowledge or rely upon God and God stands against them. That part is fairly straightforward. Grace to the humble is only obvious in its more superficial sense. The most well-known definition of grace is 'unmerited favour', something we don't deserve, and that's absolutely correct - as far as it goes. There is, however, another dimension to grace, totally consistent with unmerited favour, and that is in the realm of ability. The Greek word for grace, *charis*, has to do with gifts being freely bestowed which are not earned. It is the root

33

of the more familiar word charisma - gifted. We know that the gifts of the Spirit, for instance, are not given in quite the same way we give presents. If you give me a bicycle it is mine to use as I please. I can ride it, hang it up in my garage, or if I'm cross enough, I can sell it. But the gifts of the Spirit are provided solely to empower us for service. The gift is an enablement - we are enabled to do God's will.

HE ENABLES THE HUMBLE

God gives grace to the humble - he enables and empowers those who are relying on him to operate through them. It is walking in this understanding that allows us to move humbly out of the realm of inferiority and into confidence. If I know God is committed to operating through my humanity simply because I'm available, I can have confidence. I can have confidence that I will be able to do the job, not because God is going to harness some special talent I may possess nor because I deserve it, but because all I have to do is to get out of the way and leave him room to operate.

This is the simple God-given workings of humility, the theoretical basis of a healthy self-image. It is the awareness that anything of significance happening in or through my life is of God, and living in accordance with that understanding. One may well ask why we have so much difficulty applying this simple truth. The answer lies in the distortions human nature forces upon itself, covered in the next chapter.

POINTS TO PONDER

(Or a convenient way to get the message without
having to buy the book)

1. Jesus was humble, not grovelling in inferiority, but
seeing servanthood as a responsibility of authority.

2. Jesus' security came from his relationship with the
Father and not his position with his disciples.

3. Humility is as far removed from inferiority as it is
from pride.

4. Humility is the Bible's word for a healthy self-image.

5. Humility is the awareness that anything of eternal
significance happening in or through my life is of God.

6. If Jesus said, 'By myself I can do nothing', how much
more should that be true of me?

---

1. John 13:3-5
2. Selwyn Hughes, Every Day with Jesus (Crusade for World Revival)
3. Isaiah 6:5   4. Isaiah 6:6-9   5. Acts 9:15   6. John 5:30
7. Numbers 12:3 8. Exodus 4:1   9. Exodus 4:10   10. Exodus 6:30
11. Exodus 4:13 12. Acts 7:22   13. Exodus 7:1
14. Philippians 2:3 NASB   15. James 3:13
16. Proverbs 3:34; James 4:6; I Peter 5:5

Chapter 3

HUMAN WORTH

WORMS OR JEWELS?

Proverbs 8:31 tells of Wisdom 'rejoicing in God's creation' and 'delighting in mankind' - before the fall. Is there anything about fallen humanity to delight Wisdom, and what is the worth of redeemed humanity? Christian estimates range all the way from 'a worm' to 'more than the crown jewels' with very little in between. Are we saying: 'For God so loved the worms...'? Would God send his Son to die for people with no more value than worms? The answer to this last question is an unequivocal yes! Any other answer would imply God had some profit motive to his investment. Hence the hymn line, 'Would he devote that sacred head for such a worm as I?' It was pure grace, no more, no less.

Does God see his children as worms? The answer is an unequivocal no! There are Scriptures which are used to support 'the worm theory' certainly; the strongest is Psalm 22:6, considered by most to be the Lord Jesus on the cross saying 'I am a worm and not a man'. Jesus felt like a worm having all the sin of the world heaped upon him (that's understandable). The statement doesn't equate man and worm, it actually does the opposite, it contrasts them. God had already created worms when he made Adam, he didn't need any more.

37

I recently saw a rusty old car body, that many would have paid to have removed from their property, sell for £2,500 in a classic car auction. The worth of an item would seem to be in the eye of the purchaser. Others weren't willing to pay that much. When the wreck was sitting in someone's pasture it was of dubious value, possibly it was even seen as a liability, but the person with £2,500 had plans for it. Whether the car was worth it is insignificant, it now has an imputed value of £2,500.

Peter tells us, 'It was not with perishable things such as silver or gold that you were redeemed from the empty way of life handed down to you from your forefathers, but with the precious blood of Christ, a lamb without blemish or defect'.[2] Were we worth it? No, but we now have an imputed worth to go along with our imputed righteousness. Graham Kendrick has a line in one of his songs, 'Would you say that a man is worth nothing until someone is willing to pay?' Or, as Martin Luther is reputed to have said, 'God doesn't love us because we are of worth, we are of worth because he loves us'.

In our battle against humanistic philosophy we have been so strong on the total depravity of man that many Christians have used that as the basis of their identity. But redemption means to buy back, to restore to a former state. God created man in his image and said man, along with the rest of creation, was good. Wisdom delighted over mankind and Jesus restored us to that delightful position. Does God want us to identify with fallen humanity and the empty way of life handed down to us by our forefathers, or with our restored position for which he paid so dearly?

ASSUME THE RIGHT IDENTITY

Certainly, I can't afford to forget that without Christ I am less than nothing. There are bound to be problems, however, if this forms the substance of my identity: if I identify with my pre-redemption humanity, I will behave like the person I believe I am. Fallen man knows no sense of value so he accepts his neighbour's value system. He has no concept of love so he concentrates on self, and he has no inner resources to fight against evil so he easily gives in. We can't afford to forget that we are sinners saved by grace, but neither can we afford to take our identity from the sinner half of that truth. We must instead take our identity from the saved by grace dimension. What does it mean to be a child of the king? It undoubtedly means humility; it certainly doesn't mean to take on an unredeemed, unregenerate, uncleansed identity.

One of the main sources of power for godly living, aside from the Holy Spirit himself, is the knowledge of being a member of the Royal family, with all the resources that brings. This is 'the truth which sets us free'.[3] One of the greatest sources of defeat in the Christian life is assuming the wrong identity.

Paul addressed this very directly:

> I know that nothing good lives in me, that is, in my sinful nature. For I have the desire to do what is good, but I cannot carry it out. For what I do is not the good I want to do; no, the evil I do not want to do - this I keep on doing. Now if I do what I do not want to do, it is no longer I who do it, but it is sin living in me that does it.[4]

He addresses the total worthlessness of fallen human nature and even after discussing, at length, the crucifixion of the old nature in the previous chapter, he admits that this still causes him problems. However, the most significant factor in this passage is the source of his identity: 'Now if I do what I do not want to do, it is <u>no longer I</u> who do it, but it is sin living in me that does it' (my underlining). Why is it no longer Paul? Because Paul is a new creation. In addition to admitting that he still had problems with his old nature, he is saying (in effect): 'I no longer identify with my sinful nature, I am my new nature'.

If we identify with our old nature, believing that is the 'real us', then when we do commit ourselves to improvement, all our efforts will be directed towards our old nature. We will be polishing up something God has already condemned. The fact is, we are helpless to clean up our old nature - if we could, Christ died for nothing. Victory doesn't come through burnishing our sin nature but by putting it to death. It is not cleaning up the old nature, but walking in the new.

I can remember not too long after I was converted, hearing a speaker quoting 2 Corinthians 5:17: 'Therefore, if anyone is in Christ, he is a new creation; the old has gone, the new has come!' My inner reaction was something to the effect of 'That's easy for you to say'. I had changed to some degree, but not a lot of the old had gone, most of it was right there ready to take over. Not only was there too much of the old still about, but I wasn't sure just how much of the new was genuine. Ever ask yourself 'How much of this changed life is a new creation and how much is group conformity behaviour' (trying to fit in with my Christian friends)? With these questions in the back of my mind this verse sounded much more like what ought to be than a statement of fact: 'Now that you are in Christ you're supposed to be completely new'. I'm afraid that all too many see 2 Corinthians 5:17 the same way I did as a teenager and for a couple of decades after that.

The fact that my acceptance of being 'a new creation' was mainly academic (I accepted the doctrine) didn't make it a reality in my life. In Christian jargon, I had accepted it with my head but not my heart.

The Bible uses 'heart' as the centre of our being, but frequently uses more visceral terms when emphasizing emotions, with statements such as: 'My bowels are troubled, my liver is poured upon the earth.'[5] It may be more accurate to make the distinction between believing a fact at head level and at gut level.

I am not making a case for going on feelings, quite the contrary, but the fact remains that a lot of our actions, and most of our reactions, originate at gut level. I also believe we can, at least partially, educate our emotions. That, however, falls into the area of strategy, and although we have completed our look at God in this first area, we have only begun to look at man, so we aren't quite ready to develop a strategy.

INNER LONGINGS MET IN CHRIST

Among the many theories of personality development the idea of 'basic needs' continually emerges. It is commonly accepted that we are born with needs for security and significance. Security is defined as 'love that doesn't have to be earned'. Christian psychologist Larry Crabb recognises the importance of this secure type of love and significance, but would rather refer to them as crucial longings. He defines crucial longings as 'those desires that must be met if life is to be worth living'.[6] He refrains from the term 'needs' in order to avoid being linked with some of the classic theories associated with 'needs' for security and significance.[7]

Does the Bible support the idea that humans are born with deep inner longings for love and significance? I believe it does, primarily because these longings are met in Christ. He loves us with a love that does not have to be earned. In fact the Bible makes it very clear that he loved us enough to die in our place while we were powerless and ungodly.[8] The fact that he has prepared good works in advance for us to do,[9] given us the ministry of reconciliation,[10] and has selected us to bear fruit that will last,[11] tells us we have been allowed significant responsibility in God's business, just as Adam had before the Fall.

Not only are these inner longings met in Christ, there are quite a number of commands given to believers requiring us to love and respect others. Evidently, God wants to involve believers in meeting these longings, at certain levels, for each other.

It is extremely interesting that one of the central marriage passages, Ephesians 5, requires husbands to love their wives and wives to respect their husbands. We believe this is because with most men, the longing for significance is greater than that for love and the situation is reversed in women. Most women feel their longings for love are stronger than those for significance. God doesn't love us because we deserve it but because we need it, and he wants us to give love and respect to each other on the same basis.

When these longings go unmet, life is meaningless indeed. People feel little or no sense of self-worth and spend a lot of conscious or unconscious effort attempting to have these longings fulfilled. This may sound like a contradiction in terms, having said these deep longings are met in Christ, but it's like anything else: if we are unaware of or fail to appropriate a gift, it is of no benefit. These deep inner longings are not our only longings, but

43

they are our deepest longings and the ones that only God can fill.

Professor Eugene Peterson of Regent College Vancouver, cuts the same pie in a slightly different shape discussing intimacy and transcendence.

> Intimacy: we want to experience human love and trust and joy. Transcendence: we want to experience divine love and trust and joy. We do not become ourselves by ourselves. We do not become more human, more ourselves, when we are behind the wheel of a BMW.[12]

He believes that not only are these longings not fulfilled in our materialistic society, he gives a perfectly good reason why they can't be. He claims '...a thoroughly secularized culture is a corpse'. He perceives that intimacy in particular is a highly sought after commodity: 'Most anything at hand that gives a feeling of closeness - whether genitals or cocaine - will do for intimacy'.[13] When we hear Pascal's expression of a God-shaped void inside every human - that is it, and a mere human 'feeling of closeness' won't fill it.

WHERE DO YOU LEAN YOUR LADDER?

The two main authorities on fulfilling these longings are the experiences of life and the Bible. Unfortunately, the first has greater accessibility than television, but even less accuracy. The experiences of life pump out

44

ambiguous emotional messages which imprint themselves on our memory in a way which seems to have an iron grip on our future. For instance much of life's strategy may be developed around the way in which at age four, we interpreted remarks of our mother, or at a later stage comments made by a school teacher.

Consciously or unconsciously we will set goals to meet what we believe to be our needs. These goals will be based upon certain suppositions of what it takes to feel secure and significant. This will probably involve winning the love and respect of others.

These suppositions come mainly from inaccurate emotional files of years gone by. The things we suppose under such circumstances are not too complex:

> I suppose people will respect me and I will feel significant if I achieve.., or

> If I amass a fortune, or, am promoted ahead of my contemporaries.

> I will be loved if I invest enormous amounts of time in others, assume responsibility for ..., or

> If I am able to please. If I am never late, never wrong, always know the answer. If I always have things in perfect order, always have the right response, am always considerate, responsive and sensitive, then people will love and respect me.

We work very hard to get to the top of whatever ladder to success we have chosen. After fighting, rung by rung, to get to the top many will still not be able to shake the emptiness deep down inside. It is not difficult to cite examples of celebrities and stars who have reached the zenith of their careers and committed suicide, proving that success and successful living are two different things.

There is little benefit in being a successful ladder climber if the ladder has been placed against the wrong wall! The ladder often gets placed against the wrong wall through the emotional messages of the past. A father knowing his daughter has greater potential says: 'A 'B' would be acceptable for some girls but next, time you come home with an 'A''. Which she interprets: 'I'm only loved when I get top marks'. This and a lot of other similar remarks places her ladder against the wrong wall, and this girl grows up to be a workaholic. Who's fault is it? Such remarks are not exactly child abuse, although they certainly are unskilled parenting. It would undoubtedly remove all danger of over-population if unskilled parenting were a capital crime. She bore some of the responsibility at the time for arriving at the worst possible interpretation of 'next time come home with an 'A''.

Much more importantly, as an adult woman she bears full responsibility for her present life strategy. We are all responsible for re-examining our values from time to time. There has been a lot of energy expended in promoting the idea that we are helpless victims of our past, but that simply isn't so. Through careful training, animals can be programmed to be responsible, but animals cannot be responsible for their programming -

humans can. And God has provided all the necessary information.

We have viewed a part of God's plan and considered some of the quirks of human nature that seem to block the effective implementation of that plan. It is possible now to develop some strategy to cut through the hang-ups and build truth into our lives, which we will do in the next chapter.

POINTS TO PONDER

(Or a special condensed version for fellow dyslexics)

1. God definitely does not view the crowning jewel in his creation as a load of worms. Had he wanted more worms he surely would have started a worm farm and saved all the parental heartache of Adam, Eve and the rest of us.

2. The Bible does not equate mankind with worms, it does just the opposite, it contrasts them.

3. God doesn't love us because we are of worth, but we definitely have worth because he loves us.

4. We have imputed worth just as we have imputed righteousness.

47

5. Redemption means restoration to the former state, where God said of man along with the rest of his creation, 'It is good'.

6. The truth that sets me free is the fact that I am a new creation and no longer need to take my identity from my old nature but from the new.

7. Much of our behaviour is motivated by deep inner longings for love and to have some sort of impact on our world.

    a. The good news is that these longings are fulfilled in Christ.

    b. The bad news is that most of us look everywhere else to have them fulfilled.

1. Cartoon is from Barbara Johnson Splashes of Joy (Word, Inc., 1992) Page 70 Used with permission.
2. I Peter 1:18-19   **3**. John 8:32   **4**. Romans 7:18-20
5. Lamentations 2:11 AV. Many other such visceral examples in the Authorised Version are translated in the NIV as *compassion, distress* and *anguish* - emotions.
6. Larry Crabb, Inside Out (Nav Press page 81)
7. The hierarchy of needs theory popularised by Drs. Adler and Maslow states, basically, that one cannot become a complete person until all of one's needs are met in sequence from the basic to the highest. While most Christians would accept that we have a deep longing for love and significance, few would totally accept either Adler's or Maslow's theories.
8. Romans 5:6 **9**. Ephesians 2:10 **10**. 2 Corinthians 5:18 **11**. John 15:16
12. Eugene H. Peterson, Christianity Today (Spirit Quest) pp27-30, 8 Nov 93. Eugene H Peterson is Professor of Spiritual Theology at Regent College, Vancouver.
13. op.cit

Chapter 4

EDUCATING THE EMOTIONS

We live in a very peculiar age when even some of the best educated people believe they have scientific grounds to justify being ruled by their emotions rather than their intellect. Many would maintain they were being hypocritical to go against their feelings. Others believe it may even be dangerous. C.S. Lewis felt this notion could not coexist with Christian faith, at least not as he defined it, which was:

Faith is the art of holding on to things our reason has once accepted in spite of our changing moods. [1]

He held that a person could be successful at nothing if he allowed his emotions to control him. Yet, we all frequently have difficulty persuading our adult emotions to accept facts understood by most school children. We can know Jesus loves 'all the little children of the world' and yet function as if we were excluded. Most of us find it difficult to change the way we feel about particular issues. Some find it is easier to change their minds than their feelings. Could it be that we just don't think objectively enough about the issues that affect us?

DOING SIX THINGS AT ONCE

We have mechanisms which allow us to function quite effectively through 'force of habit'. These are good, because they allow us to do several things at once. We can drive a car while holding a conversation, enjoying the scenery, appreciating music on the car radio and possibly smoking a cigarette.

There is a certain robot quality about these mechanisms which allows us to delegate mundane tasks to them while we focus our minds on more important things. It is easy enough to operate on 'auto-pilot' to the extent that these mechanisms begin to interfere with our life. Supposing this multi-talented person wants to give up smoking? He or she may find the urge to light up is exceptionally strong when driving along enjoying good music, scenery etc. The robot begins to rule the master.

Our attitudes are similar mechanisms. Dictionary definitions of *attitude* speak of things like 'orientation of the mind, direction' and 'position'. I suspect 'preliminary file' might be even more appropriate. A word like 'abortion' calls up a preliminary file, which contains mainly emotions and a few cliches, which supposedly represent an overview of the more in-depth information contained in the intellectual file. The first problem is that the preliminary (or attitude) file, which is suppos-edly a brief and highly accessible summary of the intellectual file, is seldom kept up-to-date with the file it represents. The second problem is, few ever get past the attitude before reacting to a given provocation. They are on auto-pilot.

Forgive me if I make attitudes sound like culprits, they aren't, they are very effective servants, but they have to be kept up-to-date with the facts.

Attitudes are the mental (or cognitive) link between emotions and behaviour.

As such, they are the key to educating our emotions and regulating our behaviour. It probably is inaccurate to compare attitudes with a piece of electronic equipment which is dormant until stimulated. Attitudes may be much more biological in nature, having a life of their own. Left unattended they will behave exactly like a garden and become overgrown with weeds. Either way, attitude problems are not to be blamed on the attitude mechanism any more than garden problems can be blamed on the garden.

According to the Bible, we are the gardeners, we are responsible:

> You were taught, with regard to your former way
> of life, to put off your old self, which is being
> corrupted by its deceitful desires; to be made new
> in the attitude of your minds... [2]

51

A Humble Confidence

We have a model:

> Your attitude should be the same as that of Christ Jesus.[3]

And the resources:

> For the word of God is living and active. Sharper than any double-edged sword, it penetrates even to dividing soul and spirit, joints and marrow; it judges the thoughts and attitudes of the heart. [4]

For example, let's assume that we now intellectually accept the following:

> God opposes the proud but enables the humble.

> Humility is the understanding that anything of eternal significance happening in or through my life is of God.

> I really am a new creation - I am not my old nature, I am a new person.

But, my feelings tell me otherwise:

> God enables the humble so that must exclude me. But somebody certainly seems to be enabling the proud, yet that doesn't seem to include me either.

> Humility seems little more than being 'limp wristed'.

> And I definitely don't feel like a new creation.

As stated, I already believe the facts and they are comforting while I am actually reading them or hearing them in a sermon. But when it comes to the crunch, suppose I am easily frightened, discouraged or depressed. This may be common but it need not be accepted as normal. I can take responsibility for my attitude.

With responsibility comes hope.

At this point it might pay to contrast the thrust of Jesus' teaching with that of his contemporaries and even with the Old Testament. He acknowledged the need for right actions but he emphasized right attitudes:

> You have heard it said... 'Do not murder...' But I tell you that anyone who is angry with his brother...[5]

Certainly anger is an emotion and quite a normal one at that, so we get the idea that Jesus is not condemning the transitory emotion of anger but rather a mental orientation of anger - the attitude. The emotion is seldom under our direct control but the attitude is. This is because attitudes don't just flash up on the screens of our minds the way emotions do, they are developed. We are responsible for their development. This is even more clearly demonstrated in Jesus' teaching on adultery:

> You have heard it said, 'Do not commit adultery.' But I tell you that anyone who looks at a woman lustfully...'[6]

Ideas, like emotions, just seem to arrive, they flit into our

53

minds, often completely uninvited. There is an old paraphrase of this passage which goes: 'It's no sin for a bird to land on your head, but you don't have to let him make a nest there'. Sexual thoughts will come and go but we can't afford to develop an attitude of adultery. We may not comprehend an attitude of adultery being as grave a sin as the physical act, but one thing is certain, our attitudes are soon betrayed in our actions.

Attitudes authorise actions.

Allowing ourselves develop an attitude of adultery sets our seal of approval on the act. The only thing that stands between us and the act is the opportunity and the fear of being caught. It is not within the scope of this book to avoid the snares of overt sins like murder and adultery (as noble as that would be), but to demonstrate how the same dynamics are involved in the much more covert sin of simply not taking God at his word. This surely robs us of our inheritance just as much as social sins.

AS A MAN THINKS...

The fact that our actions follow our attitudes would be reason enough for Jesus to emphasise attitudes, but a more important factor is that we are what we think - not the doctrines to which we give mental assent, but the attitudes we cultivate.

Our intellectual files all tell us God is good. Satan's main objective is to cast doubt on that.

It is difficult for him to insert this into a believer's intellectual file, but attitudes that 'God isn't good enough to be concerned with this' are all too common.

The material in an intellectual file doesn't really become a part of us until it is updated into the appropriate attitude file, and it is our attitude files which govern the majority of our actions and almost all of our reactions. The positive side of Jesus' condemnation of sinful attitudes is the fact that it indicates that we actually do have control over them. We will explore this area of responsibility more fully later.

The very fact of bearing responsibility can be harnessed to our advantage with regard to our self-image. It is the first step to educating our emotions and regulating our behaviour. If the first step is the understanding that with responsibility comes hope, the second is the knowledge that self-control is actually listed under the fruit of the Spirit. It is not a gift of the Spirit such as healing and prophecy which are given to some and not to others. It is a manifestation of the fruit of the Spirit along with love, joy and peace, so we know it is readily available to all of us.

As I have already stated, it is difficult for our intellect to have direct communication with our emotions, they just aren't on speaking terms. Ever try to talk yourself out of being scared? You may have succeeded in behaving like you weren't. The chances are that even that success was the result of being even more scared of the consequences of not behaving bravely. Both intellect and emotions have equal access to our attitudes which in turn controls the majority of our behaviour. This means that we need a lot of messages travelling from the intellect to the attitude file.

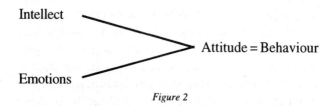

Figure 2

How do we know when we are communicating with our attitudes rather than our emotions or behaviour? When we do it in advance of the problem! Meditation on the Scriptures both crystallises our intellectual grasp of a given principle and adds powerful resources to the attitude files. This self-programming provides an accurate data base for godly reactions to life situations. We can update the attitude file prior to experience. For example, an effective working awareness that my Heavenly Father is actually in control of which painful remarks reach my ears, allows me to respond with much greater patience. I save myself a lot of agro I when remember that devaluing remarks are made by people who have a need to do so. But it definitely takes some disciplined attitude file maintenance to remember this <u>before</u> I get upset.

RENEWING THE MIND

Emotions have a good deal of their input into attitudes during emergencies, and the emotional data stays in place to be reinforced at the next scare. We must communicate to our attitudes in advance of the problem. During the emergency the emotions are talking so loudly that little else can be heard. If there is clear, current intellectual data in the attitude file which has recently been reinforced, there is a far better chance the intellect will win out. Psychologists currently call this pre-storing of intellectual data *self-talk*. However, it is entirely consistent with what we read in Scripture. For instance, we know that David was continually speaking to himself and even sorting out what he was going to say, such as: 'Why are you downcast, O my soul? Why are you so disturbed within me? Put your hope in God, for I will yet praise him, my saviour and my God'. [7] Christians above any other group of people should profit from self-talk because we have a firm base of truth from which to function.

We are all familiar with Paul's admonition to present ourselves 'as living sacrifices', and that it is followed by, 'Do not conform any longer to the pattern of this world, but be transformed by the renewing of your mind'. [8] The terminology of Ephesians 4:23, 'the attitudes of your minds', drives home the point that attitudes are very much matters of the mind. Consequently, we can view the renewing of our attitudes not only as a scriptural command (which carries with it all of the necessary resources), but an absolute necessity in the whole process of developing a biblically based self-image.

Certainly this admonition to renew our minds is very much an exhortation to release ourselves from a secular world view. Possibly the most famous quote of J.B. Phillips[9] comes from his translation of Romans 12:2, 'Don't let the world around you squeeze you to its own mould'. Not only is this passage about the competition between godly and secular influences on our minds, it is also in the context of self-image. The very next verse specifically addresses it.

For by the grace given me I say to every one of you: Do not think of yourself more highly than you ought, but rather think of yourself with sober judgment, in accordance with the measure of faith God has given you.[10]

A FACTUAL FRAMEWORK

J.B. Phillips translates sober judgement as 'sane estimate', Jay Adams emphasizes accuracy,[11] both of which, in this context, mean an appraisal uncontaminated by godless values. As previously suggested, a truly accurate self-image can only be developed within a framework of authoritative information on the character of God and the nature of man.

Consequently, the first steps in ensuring an accurate

self-image are to ensure the framework is intact, intellectually. Have I a firm grasp on the fact that a sound self-image is based on a relationship with God? Am I conscious that God desires to reach others through that relationship, and that any significant accomplishment in my life will be of him? Am I intellectually convinced that I am actually a new creation? C.S. Lewis' definition of faith (previously cited) as 'holding on to the things our reason has once accepted', is not all that different than Hebrews 11:1 on that score. Hebrews speaks of 'being sure of what we hoped for' and it isn't using hope to mean a desire, but a conviction. I find when the chips are down the only thing that keeps me going is a well-considered conviction of my position in Christ.

As a dyslexic, in the days before the educational world had recognised the condition, I didn't have the educational potential that can be expected by young people today in the same situation. I make it no secret that I am short on formal education. Although I don't believe anyone seriously considers me uneducated, I do occasionally find myself in situations where subtle attempts are made to use this as a point of leverage to carry a particular argument. For instance, when others on a committee with more liberal views of Scripture have difficulty reasoning with me, it may be implied that it is due to a lack of sophistication on my part.

Let me tell you, this is not without effect on me. It has the effect of making me want to fold up and 'go back where I belong'. Or to where whoever made the remark would like me to believe I belong. I am not impervious to being snubbed, and it hurts. But I don't back down because I realise this is exactly where I belong, standing nose to nose with this guy who has to draw strength from his credentials because he can't defend his position from Scripture and logic. Often there are people depending on me to make sure the Christian position is clear and unadulterated. But I can only hang in there because of the convictions I have regarding my position with my Father. I know he didn't recruit me because of my qualifications, he simply commissioned me to be available to all he wants to accomplish in and through me. Having no academic credentials is a definite handicap, but his strength is manifested through my weakness.

I realise, looking over the past two paragraphs, that they could sound courageous, because we think of standing in the face of intimidating opposition (and intimidated is an accurate description of my feelings) as raw courage. That is not an unreasonable definition of courage, but I'm not speaking as one who has courage of his own. My message is that God provides the courage, I just have to have it filed where I can find it when it is required.

EMERGENCY PROCEDURES

The obvious next step is to ensure that the attitude files are amended to reflect this understanding. I would first look at all the Scriptures pertaining to things like humility and identity. This will also serve to verify my intellectual position. This is where Scripture memory proves invaluable. Every aircraft crew member, from stewardess to pilot, commercial, private or military, has to memorize certain emergency procedures. These consist of the most important actions they would take in the event of an emergency such as loss of cabin pressure, hydraulic pressure or an engine fire. All crew members are subject to be quizzed on these emergency procedures on a 'no notice' basis. The obvious reason for this is the fact that there isn't time to look through a manual when action is necessary NOW. There are no passengers in God's economy, we're all crew members. Undoubtedly, our list of emergency procedures should begin with a bold type statement:

God is good - regardless of what the circumstances seem to be telling me.

But we will quickly require scriptural authority for specific back-up in varying circumstances.

I know Scripture memory sounds rote and boring as well as hard work. It doesn't have to be. In the first place, it isn't necessary to memorize masses of texts, only the one or two you select as providing the strongest case. Secondly, it is not necessary to memorize the entire verse. The Navigators may not be too pleased with this idea, but you must remember verse numbers were only assigned to locate information, not as the exact parameters of a specific thought. Even the Navs will admit that verses begin and end in peculiar places.

Another thing that may be helpful when memorising texts for our attitude file is to amplify the message. This can be done safely and easily by comparing translations and using the one which most powerfully speaks of the subject you are most concerned with. There is nothing wrong with this. Most expository preaching consists of some chap showing us all we should be able to extract from a given passage. And, some translations serve one verse better than they do another. A good Bible teacher may provide additional help if he or she can recognise that a given source word in the original language can be translated in several ways.

An example of shortening would be 1 Peter 5:5, a verse we discussed at the end of chapter two: 'Young men, in the same way be submissive to those who are older. All of you, clothe yourselves with humility toward one another, because, "God opposes the proud but gives grace to the humble"'.

Which do you feel conveys the point, 'clothe yourselves with humility towards one another, because, "God opposes the proud but gives grace to the humble"', or simply 'God opposes the proud but gives grace to the humble'? As I said in chapter two, this last statement appears in Proverbs 3:34 and James 4:6; in neither place do just those words appear by themselves, but that is all the information I feel is crucial for my attitude file. Personally I have it on file for attitude purposes as, 'God opposes the proud but he *enables* the humble'. This is a good example of amplifying. I have streamlined the passage, using only the core message, and I have amplified that message by emphasizing the enabling dimension of grace.

INDEXING THE MIND

Many people, such as my wife and I, who do a lot of travelling and conducting seminars have certain things ready to go all the time. We don't want to have to pack a toilet kit every weekend so we keep one ready to go. This means duplication of most items but it is worth it in time saved. We also have our notes and overhead projector slides in folders neatly arranged in a file for quick accessibility. The material can be altered from group to group, but the core information is there available to meet the need.

Developing right attitudes does the same thing with our minds. Using the strategy of memorizing Scripture we place the information on file; by reviewing it we keep it accessible. The most important part of this strategy is to remember that it develops attitudes. It isn't designed to deny emotions, or simply learn doctrine or principles. It is designed to index the mind, providing easy access to the most crucial truths.

We review it most effectively through meditation. There is plenty written on meditation, but the idea of 'ruminating', chewing the cud, describes the basic process. It is important that we satisfy ourselves that we understand the meaning of the verse in its context. Then we can ruminate over possible applications in current situations, such as, 'How does this verse apply to the interaction I had with my boss this morning?' Scripture memory alone will not build godly attitudes, it can only provide an accurate value basis. It is this quest for application (generally through meditation) which creates godly attitudes and builds confidence as we become adept at applying God's Word in practical situations.

Having a grasp on all that we are in Christ and the fact that this is our true identity goes a long way towards a firm basis for our self-image, but these are not the only hurdles. There are still other factors which allow outside forces to control our lives. We will be using the same formula of looking to God rather than man to develop a strategy.

POINTS TO PONDER

(When you're stuck at a traffic light)

1. We live in a society which seems to be saying, 'If there is a conflict between our thoughts and our emotions, it's better to change our minds than our feelings.'

2. Attitudes, like money, make good servants but poor masters. They need to be under our control.

3. Attitudes are the mental link between our emotions and our behaviour. The only way to ensure our feelings don't control our actions is to develop right attitudes.

4. Attitudes are a lot like gardens, and the Bible tells us we are the gardeners - we are responsible.

5. The Sermon on the Mount demonstrates the tremendous sin potential of our attitudes. We are what we think.

6. Psychologists have coined the term 'self-talk' which is actually a very biblical concept. It can be a way of firming up our convictions to ensure the world around us doesn't squeeze us into its mould.

7. Memorizing Scriptures is the best way to develop credible 'emergency procedures'.

8. God is good - in spite of what the circumstances seem to be telling me.

1. C.S. Lewis, <u>Mere Christianity</u> (Fount Paperbacks) 21st impression, Dec 1985, page 121
2. Ephesians 4:22-23   **3**. Philippians 2:5   **4**. Hebrews 4:12
5. From Matthew 5:21-22 **6**. From Matthew 5:27-28
7. Psalm 42:5   **8**. Romans 12:1-2
9. J.B. Phillips, New Testament in Modern English. Geoffrey Bles, London
10. Romans 12:3
11. <u>The Biblical View of Self-Esteem, Self-Love, Self-Image</u>, chapter 11 - Plus many of his lectures.

Chapter 5

ON AUTO-PILOT

There are two general ways in which individuals with deep seated self-image problems are often viewed. The first is as unfortunate victims of an irreversible sequence of events. They are considered to have spiralled so deeply as to possess nowhere near the necessary strength to oppose the process. They are seen as hopeless.

The second perspective may initially seem much less compassionate, as it implies that a poor self-image is considered, at least partially, to be an improper response to the difficulties of life. This is not simply labelling it 'a self-inflicted wound', it is actually the most optimistic outlook. It is the only view that offers any hope.

ACTING OUT A SCRIPT?

If life amounts to nothing more than acting out a script written for us by our parents, teachers and peers, then we are certainly not responsible. However, when someone with a poor self-image recognises which aspects of the problem are actually under their control, they gain hope. This is, of course, the reason for writing this book - to give hope.

Hope, gained through insight to individual responsibility, can be a bitter pill to swallow, but it bears the greatest promise.

To say the emotional damage from any amount or degree of sins committed against us cannot be put right is to limit the gospel. We are told 'the blood of Jesus, his Son, purifies us from all sin'.[1] That covers the sins committed against us as well as those sins for which we are responsible. As with a lot of other problems, counsel, support and encouragement are helpful in reclaiming lost ground, but in the end it is the individual's relationship with God and his or her obedience that makes the crucial difference.

Things said and done to us when we are young and vulnerable are often taken on board as deep hurts. These words and actions colour our perspective on life leaving us with twisted interpretations of events. And so the spiral goes. But, if an individual has come to Christ they have made at least one correct response in their life and that has empowered them to make additional right decisions. As we discuss wrong decisions and the gospel's ability to pick up the pieces, please limit your imagination to self-image problems, because that is the scope of this book.[2]

TRUTH = FREEDOM

Jesus said: 'If you hold to my teaching, you are really my disciples. Then you will know the truth, and the truth

67

will set you free'.³ The truth sets us free, and we know the truth as the result of holding to his teaching. Once we begin to apply the bits we understand, we get more understanding, more truth and greater freedom. As with any biblical principle, a 'nuts and bolts' approach is required and we have already entered into this to some degree.

Our attitudes are the area where we do have control. I don't wish to imply that changing attitudes is easy, but we have the assurance that any place where God demands change he also provides the power to do so. A classic example of this is Galatians 5:19-23 which lists the works of the flesh and the fruit of the Spirit. It makes an interesting study. At least five of the sixteen acts of our sinful nature are clearly attitudes and all nine of the qualities listed as the fruit of the Spirit fall in the category of attitudes.

Forgiving those who sin against us is demanded and bitterness is condemned. Both forgiveness and bitterness are attitudes. Agape love, which is identified in several texts as the key attribute of godliness, is first and foremost an attitude of selfless commitment to others.⁴

Our minds are a lot like computers in that they can be programmed. Our attitudes are the actual programme files. Computers contain numerous files that do nothing but store information, but they are not the programme files. Our minds are similar. For example, I have several people's birthdays on file in my mind (as information), but the way I respond to this information is determined by my attitude towards the person. I may feel that we no longer have sufficient contact to warrant the sending of presents. Attitudes are the place where the programming of minds is actually accomplished. This is why it is necessary to meditate on Scripture, rather than just to memorise it. Scripture becomes a part of us and the ethical basis for our 'programming' or attitude files only when we meditate on it, otherwise it remains just more data.

The question is, who should I allow to programme my mind? Can I actually allow just anyone to place their fingers on the buttons of my brain? The answer is obviously no! The reason it is 'no', is that I am responsible for my attitudes. As previously discussed, the Sermon on the Mount tells us of the Lord's concern with attitudes. When I stand before the judgement seat of Christ, the majority of issues under review will be my attitudes. I won't be able to blame my bitterness against an individual on the fact that they offended me. The sin of bitterness is on my record not theirs. By one offensive act I have, in effect, allowed them to program my mind, but I am responsible.

ASSUMING RESPONSIBILITY

Have you ever considered the basic issue at stake in the parable of the talents in Matthew 25:14-30? Verse 15 gives a key fact. 'To one he gave five talents of money, to another two talents, and to another one talent, each according to his ability. Then he went on his journey.' The important thing is that the master entrusted each according to what he knew was their level of ability. The first two made wise investments and doubled their money, but the man with only one talent made none. The best he felt he could do was to keep it secure. After all, there is some risk in investing, but there was evidently more risk in doing nothing because the master called him wicked and lazy, and had him punished.

The problem revolves around two different assessments of the man's abilities, that of his master (which represents the Lord's assessment and is therefore accurate) and the man's own assessment. Would the Lord punish a person for too low an assessment of their own ability? That is not exactly what happened. The parable leads one to believe that the master believed the man could have doubled his one talent. Verse 27 tells us the master would have viewed even the normal bank rate interest as acceptable, but the man didn't even do that. The thing he was being punished for was failure to assume responsibility.

The master had entrusted him with the stewardship of a large sum of money and he allowed his fear to neutralise any ability he did have. Fear is not a punishable offence, but allowing fear to stop us performing our duties is irresponsible or even cowardice, both of which are punishable.

Where did the fear come from? An inaccurate assessment of his ability. We don't know where the low estimate came from, but it was most likely someone telling him he had no business getting involved in the investment market without the proper education or at least an old school tie. If he paid attention to that kind of talk he was allowing someone else to programme his mind. Who got punished? It wasn't the guy who was pressing his buttons - the servant himself was punished. He was responsible for his attitude of inferiority.

SELF-TALK

Telling ourselves the truth is pretty much a full-time job, especially if we have had a lot of faulty programming. Even if we have had a good start in life through a wonderful childhood, telling ourselves the truth is a very high priority vigil. It is claimed that we speak to ourselves at the rate of 1,300 words per minute. That may, at first glance, sound a bit far fetched, but think about it for a minute and it seems quite plausible. Think of all that flashes through our mind as we encounter the experiences of life. Part of the process of interpreting them and determining the significance of each involves a replay of what we believe to be similar situations. When you think of all the data running through and the amount of space that would be required to write it all down, 1,300 words per minute doesn't sound the least bit over the top. Naturally one has to talk fast to get it all in, because it's something like a perpetual news broadcast - with commentary.

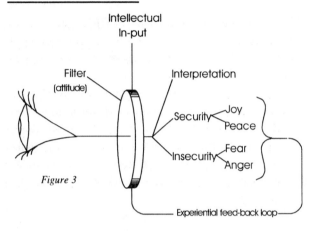

Figure 3

Here we have a filter - another metaphor for an attitude. Every life experience is filtered through the attitudes we develop. Each experience is first of all interpreted to determine if it contributes to our security or detracts from it. Then, depending on the interpretation, suitable emotions are produced. The emotions are then fed back to become a part of the attitude. As you can see there is an 'experiential feed-back loop' which ensures that each experience contributes to the filter effect and the filter influences our interpretation of each experience.

THERE'S NO ACCOUNTING FOR TASTE

It works something like this. A woman made an apple pie and a chocolate pie. Her guests complimented her on the apple pie, but absolutely raved about the chocolate pie. Her interpretation was, 'I am good at chocolate pies but not so good at apple'. When she had another go at the apple pie, her husband complimented her on it, but asked how soon she would make another chocolate pie. This was interpreted as, 'why don't you give up on apple pies?' And this was duly recorded in her attitude file.

The question is how much of what we say to ourselves is the product of the experiential feedback loop and how much is intellectual input? The experiential loop is working all the time, it is automatic. This means it is extremely important that we have a reasonable amount of intellectual input, because if we don't we are just running on 'auto pilot'.

It is obvious that the purpose of this experiential loop is that we should learn through our experiences. We are (to use our computer analogy again) self-programming. The thinking has been that if the early programming was good, future interpretations of life would be accurate and therefore future self-programming would also be accurate and so forth. This is not a new idea. To quote Solomon: 'Train a child in the way he should go, and when he is old he will not turn from it'.[5] Conversely, if early programming was faulty so the interpretations of life experiences would be faulty, as would be the subsequent programming. Inaccurate programming leads to more inaccurate programming.

This could give the impression that once effective self-programming is in place we could go through life on auto-pilot, never having to think again. Indeed, some people never do - at least they never seem to question the implications of their beliefs, attitudes and actions. But

the fact is, no one has had such accurate initial programming that their experience loop will function unaided for
very long without inaccuracies creeping in and then
multiplying. Adding accurate information corrects the
distortions; the truth sets us free from distortion. However, to rest in the fact that we have made corrections is
like resting in the fact that we once took a bath.

Our values are under constant attack, and not always
from head-on assaults. Often it's the oblique strikes that
go undetected. One broad consequence of this is that sin
is 'normalised' to the point that the Church has
committees pondering issues the Bible clearly calls sin.
Often they are not pondering whether they ought to love
the people involved, but whether to ordain them. Society
and the media are providing the bulk of the experiences
contributing to our attitudes. Unless we are having
accurate intellectual input as well, we are bound to be
contaminated by them. We can even have our opinion
on the value of the Bible contaminated, and unfortunately,
that is not an uncommon occurrence.

At this point I am not interested in the moral implications
of this experiential feedback, except as an illustration. I
am concerned with its self-image implications. It can
obviously have tremendous impact. 'A little leaven
leavens the whole lump',[6] and a remark wrongly interpreted can shatter confidence. But shattered confidence
can be a temporary thing covering a particular skill, or
it can be a life-dominating problem. Life-dominating
problems rob us of our birthright as they neutralise our

potential to mature and be used by the Lord.

Allowing the experiences of life to be the dominating influence in our attitudes towards values can place us in the same position as the man with the one talent - cast into outer darkness due to disobedience.

POINTS TO PONDER

(It will actually help it sink in)

1. If life amounts to nothing more than acting out a script written by the significant others in my life, then there is no hope, but as soon as I assume responsibility for the person I am, I have hope.

2. Changing our attitudes isn't always easy, but it is one area where we do have control.

3. We normally respond to life by chattering away to ourselves at a rate of 1,300 words per minute. Most of this high speed self-talk consists of replays of experiences similar to what we are experiencing at the moment plus associated information - most of which is inaccurate.

4. Talking to ourselves is a full time job, the only way to ensure the accuracy of this self-talk is to provide

deliberate factual input. Without that we are reinforcing a lot of erroneous notions.

5. We are told 'Love the Lord your God with all your heart and with all your soul and with all your mind'. Some Christians function as if true spirituality meant to run on auto pilot.

1. I John 1:7
2. It is always tempting to recall extreme psychiatric problems to challenge the applicability of Christian principles to such cases. I don't believe Christian counselling is impotent in any emotional problem and has even proven helpful in situations which are hormonal or chemical in origin. However, we must limit our focus to self-image.
3. John 8:31-32
4. Matthew 22:37-40; Romans 13:8-10; Galatians 5:6 &14. James 2:8 calls 'Love your neighbour as yourself', the Royal Law.
5. Proverbs 22:6   **6**. Galatians 5:9

Chapter 6

COMPARISON

Comparison, or relativism, is the unavoidable result of godless thinking. If one says there is no God then there are no absolute standards to judge moral or ethical behaviour, or the worth of a person. Actions are no longer right or wrong, but merely socially acceptable or unacceptable, and the worth of a person is relative to his/her neighbour. Life becomes one long competition where loving our neighbour is frequently eclipsed by our impulsive attempts to triumph over our neighbour.

Another problem which is implied in the parable of the talents (discussed in the last chapter) is comparison. The chap given five talents to invest had twenty years experience in a major finance house in the city and quite a reputation. The fellow with two had managed investments for a large insurance company over the preceding nine years, but our friend had only managed the master's account books for the past four years. It may have seemed quite natural, under the circumstances, for him to feel a bit inferior. Compared to the others he didn't have much experience. But the fact was, the master gave him a responsibility which he knew this servant could successfully complete. That part, unlike the experience levels, is no fanciful illustration.

Paul is very definite about the dangers of comparison: 'We do not dare to classify or compare ourselves with some who commend themselves. When they measure themselves by themselves and compare themselves with themselves, they are not wise'.[1] The problem is that we are switching from God's absolute values to relative values, comparison with our neighbour.

When we switch from God's absolute values to the world's relative standards we are no longer telling ourselves the truth. In fact we may become totally oblivious to the truth.

One of Satan's main levers in manipulating our self-image is to cause us to lose sight of our uniqueness. We are all too easily thrown into the 'compare, compete and conquer' mode. This, of course, is the equivalent of duping us into selling our birthright. Uniqueness is a basic quality we possess as the result of being created in the image of our unique Heavenly Father. He is not a god created in the image of man, but the God in whose image every man, woman, boy or girl that ever drew breath was created.

UNIQUE

The Bible itself, as a document, is a monument to the intended uniqueness of the individual, with approximately forty different authors all expressing the same message in different ways. The Gospels even more graphically make this point as similar incidents in the life of Jesus are narrated through four different men. It is clear that God had a purpose in having these events recorded from four slightly different perspectives, to cater to the needs of four different categories of audiences.

The Incarnation is the most unique event in history. No other god ever claimed to make himself so vulnerable as to become a baby! Several scholars have termed John 1:14 as the single most significant text in the Bible.[2] 'The Word became flesh' also means the Word became fact, because it encapsulated all of God's character and plan into a tangible person. Nothing short of the Incarnation could have saved us. The Word become flesh was also God made available, God's authentic self-revelation. E. Stanley Jones described Jesus as 'God approachable'. Jesus Christ was God's personal response to the personal cry of the human heart.[3]

The Incarnation also answers the sceptic's question, 'Does God actually care?' Not only was the Word made flesh to dwell among us, the Incarnation fleshed out specific words like, 'See I have engraved you on the palms of my hands'.[4] Jesus didn't just talk about the ninety and nine, he lived it, proving each person matters. The world saw Jesus fellowship with social outcasts, touch lepers and exercise compassion on embarrassed people like the woman with the issue of blood and the one taken in adultery. These were not just the 'nobodies', they were the people the rest of society found inconvenient - the ones they wished didn't exist. The Incarnation doesn't answer the question, 'Why does God allow this?' but it does show that each person matters and he definitely cares what happens.

The Incarnation is also God providing a model of how the Spirit of God could express himself uniquely through committed humanity.

INTERDEPENDENT

Adam and Eve were perfect humans; there isn't a career they couldn't have successfully pursued. Aptitude tests didn't apply to them as they had an aptitude for everything. They were created in the image of a perfect God. Adam and Eve's descendants, unfortunately, were created in their twisted and fallen image.

Each of us bears the marks of the Fall. Although intact in some areas, we are unmistakably twisted in others. Those with near-perfect skills in some spheres fail miserably in others. We would like to be independent, but God in his wisdom has deemed that Adam's descendants must be interdependent.

None of us has a full tool kit! Self-reliance is unrealistic, over the long term. God does not issue exclusive franchises of his power, but he does provide gifts for the benefit of his Church (the Body). This is the background of the body illustration in 1 Corinthians 12, one of the most graphic teaching metaphors in the Bible. Eyes, for instance, are definitely very special, but if every body part were an eye we would be missing hundreds of essential functions, and would be unable to exist. Value-wise it is clear that we are all equal, but not interchangeable. We are all parts of one body, totally interdependent.

But a post-Christian society, with no access to the big picture, automatically reverts to the importance of the individual member over the body. It is nearly impossible to develop a philosophy of serving others apart from the concept of serving God, therefore we become self-serving.

Rather than measure our well-being by the well-being of the group: 'My group is doing well, I am part of the group, therefore I am doing well'. We contrast our well-being with the group: 'I must be doing well, I'm ahead of my group'. Or possibly: 'It doesn't really matter so much how I am doing so long as it is better than the group'.

COMPARISON SATURATES SOCIETY

Comparison is taught early on. In school it is taught through the grading system and the playground. World class athletes are given official world rankings, they may be number 1 or number 257 but they have a ranking. Unofficially, someone is the number one golfer in our area and the golfers know who it is. This type of comparison is all around us and teaches us from an early age that our worth comes from some outside source.

Comparison creates a deficit mentality, there is not enough recognition or status to go around. Only a few can be at the top, so we have to compete with others for our self-worth. Consequently, we are not too happy to

81

see them achieving things because that means we have to work all the harder just to stand still.

Comparison is not limited to the realm of competence, social acceptance is equally as relative and competitive (although the ground rules are less clear). First we are taught our parents' version of socially acceptable behaviour; later our peers are a greater influence. Throughout life we experience affirmation or rejection. This emotional rendition of the carrot and stick is much more powerful and definitely more subtle. The stick would have hurt, but the rejection of our peers for dressing differently probably hurts even more. There is no way to avoid teaching appropriate social behaviour in a secular society,[5] and discipline is necessary, but the fact that acceptable behaviour is relative makes it hard to maintain a sense of uniqueness.

Parents play a large part in determining a child's belief system. This includes such things as the importance of acceptance, what it takes to be accepted, and which goals are important. In our secular society many parents use both comparison and the sliding scale of relativity. Added to this, many parents discipline in such a way that the child is not sure if it is him or his behaviour that is being rejected.

Determinism tells us that the script is written through our childhood - 'the child is parent to the adult'- and gives very little hope of changing the script. It is true that we did develop a certain belief system through the feedback we received from the 'significant others' in our lives. But it is not true that this system is fixed for us forever.

I am convinced that had Sigmund Freud never lived we would still view childhood as the source our troubles. Much of psychotherapy consists of restructuring faulty layers of an inadequate childhood, giving the message that happiness comes from a good childhood. Possibly a happy childhood would better equip us to cope with the 'God Shaped Void' that Pascal spoke of, or Larry Crabb's 'Hollow Core', but how effective is the restructuring of these faulty layers if the 'Hollow Core'[6] isn't satisfactorily filled? Hopefully, Christian psychotherapists work on both aspects. This void is not completely filled by inviting Jesus in as Saviour, but by making him Lord of every area of life (which we find to be more of a journey than a decision).

There is a natural law that says: 'People are not willing to listen to your solution until they're convinced you understand the problem'. Very sensible. But it also makes us very vulnerable because there is a certain therapeutic quality about being understood. People who present themselves with great empathy get a hold of our heartstrings in a way that makes us feel good, at least temporarily. Such a speaker, writer or counsellor can be very short on answers if they can convince us they understand the problem. And what better problem to 'understand' than an inadequate childhood? Targeting people with a less than optimal childhood provides access to wide open market. This focus is being 'institutionalised' with new movements and organisations emerging all the time.

The co-dependency movement is such an institution. It is an American product of the seventies, which began with a focus on children of alcoholics. They have broadened their scope to include people from all types of 'dysfunctional families'. They believe people from such families are heavily 'scripted' by the family and they want to help them to write a new script. One of their apostles, John Bradshaw, wrote 'Once a person believes that his identity lies outside himself in a substance, activity or another person, he has found a new god, sold his soul and become a slave'.[7]

ADULT CHILDREN OF NORMAL PARENTS ANNUAL CONVENTION

WELCOME ACONP MEMBERS

Some segments of secular society are becoming just a bit fed up with the notion that we are stuck with bad scripts written in our childhood and believe it is possible to rewrite them without professional help. People are being encouraged to draw on their 'inner strength' and to concentrate on developing inner character. But there is some confusion as to what this inner strength is and what exactly constitutes character.

Dr Stephen Covey defines character as 'building your security on your integrity to your value system'.[9] In other words, people have character if they are true to their own values. Sounds a bit like Polonius: 'To thine own self be true'. Well, that's a step in the right direction because a lot of people have standards for others that they don't keep themselves. But what if my values are shot full of holes. Do I still have character?

The co-dependency movement rightly encourages one to assume responsibility for one's own life, but some of its representatives portray this as a very self-centred independence. They depict a movement fuelled by an extreme hatred of all family and social structures that it believes are responsible for underprivileged childhoods. The trouble with relying on hate or anger for motivation is that we have to stay upset all the time to be successful.

NO ACTION WITHOUT MOTIVATION

What is true, unless something intervened, is that the values we learned (and the resulting belief system) channelled our motivation, if they did not become the driving force themselves. We may have been fortunate and developed a fairly accurate belief system, or maybe a faulty one. Every action is the result of some motivation, and between the motivation and the action is a belief or assumption of what it will take to satisfy that motivation.

Our basic longings for love and significance motivate us to certain actions. We don't all choose the same actions because opinions vary as to what it will take to have those longings fulfilled. If I believe my longing for significance will be fulfilled through success in athletics, (as I did as a teenager) then my goal will be to be the best possible athlete. I will work long hours, building my body and gaining the necessary skills, and it won't be for the fun of it or the love of the sport, it will be because I need to. My goal is based on what my belief system tells me will fulfil my longing for significance. It is always a matter of my personal interpretation of the messages I am receiving from society, and we are all Adult Children of a Dysfunctional Society.

Obviously this belief system is colouring my view of life because I am making a lot of assumptions about other people's actions based on my beliefs. Suppose I have been led to believe that I don't have a lot to offer socially and I invite someone to dinner, when they turn down the invitation due to a pressing work load, I may believe that was only an excuse not to get socially involved with me. I will feel the pain of rejection, not necessarily because

I was rejected, but because I thought I was. This could cause further complications: I won't ask them again because I couldn't stand being rejected again; I might even find some way of rejecting them in return. Whereas it could be that all along they wanted to come to dinner but really couldn't afford the time.

This type of scenario reinforces the message that my self-worth comes from outside myself. My life is effectively controlled by others, those on whom I depend for love, those I hope to overwhelm in the competition for significance and those whom I imagine sit on some mystical panel of judges keeping score on personal worth. If we are building our security on the inner resources developed as we are conformed to the image of Christ, rather than a deficit mentality we will develop a credit mentality - plenty for all, knowing that God wants to do exactly the same thing in all of us.

It wouldn't take much alteration of John Bradshaw's comment to provide the necessary inner resources. 'Once a person believes that his identity lies in God he is then free to commit his soul and become a slave.' Naturally, the world can't comprehend freedom through slavery to God.

LONGINGS

All behaviour is motivated by something. Regardless of our desire to please the Lord and our concern for others, a certain amount of our behaviour will be motivated by our own longings. There is nothing wrong with this provided we remember two things. The first is that the meaning and purpose of life is not to fulfil our own longings. The second is to make sure we have accurately assessed which goals we need to reach to fulfil these longings. The fact that our deepest longings for love and significance have already been met in Christ means that we are going to experience the greatest awareness of this when our efforts are expended in pleasing him. Anything less would definitely be to place our ladder against the wrong wall, because he is the only one who can actually satisfy these particular longings.

On another level we have what we call relational longings, the desire to be loved and appreciated by those close to us - parents, children, spouse, friends and colleagues. These longings are beyond our control. We can work very hard to be loved and respected by the important people in our lives, but there is no guarantee that the effort will be rewarded.

Those who don't know the Lord might see this level as the most crucial area of life, because success in this area seems to at least partially fill the emptiness resulting from unmet inner longings. The hurts suffered here frequently seem more painful than even our inner longings simply because they are more acute and piercing. But the damage done by a disease isn't always commensurate with the pain.

Surface longings entail things which, for the most part,

are under our control. This level consists of such things as our appetite for comfort, good food and sex, as well as our materialistic urges to acquire things. It includes pursuing hobbies and favourite pastimes, more creative pursuits like writing a book and preparing lessons. These longings don't have quite the potential for pain as the relational area. Most of us can endure physical discomfort more easily than rejection.

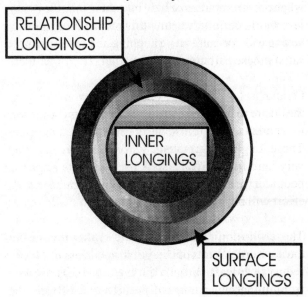

RELATIONSHIP LONGINGS

INNER LONGINGS

SURFACE LONGINGS

Figure 4 [10]

In this diagram all three levels of longings have been met. This is a Christian who has obviously been blessed. If this person were totally unaware of how truly loved and significant he/she is in Christ, the centre area would be blank, the inner longings would be unmet. What happens when problems arise in the relational area? He or she won't look for comfort from deep within, because there has never been anything but a gnawing emptiness there.

The chances are he/she will turn to the area that is under their control to numb the pain - the surface longings. They may throw themselves into their job, they may sleep more, drink more, smoke more, and/or eat more in their search for comfort. Shopping and entertainment become standard cure-alls, for anything from loneliness to depression.

Dealing with the pain of unfulfilled longings is only half of the story. There is also the question of a strategy for having these longings satisfied. We can rest assured that an individual who is not looking to God for the deep sense of love and significance which comes from him, will be strongly motivated to have their relational longings realized and will frequently manipulate others to do so. Their efforts will be directed by their value system, but not necessarily the values they hold intellectually. It will be the values and beliefs on file as attitudes. Those who recognise that there is actually a difference between the two files may blame it on the scripting of their childhood. Unfortunately, there can be absolutely no hope for a person until they assume responsibility for keeping their attitude files in line with what they have accepted intellectually as truth.

POINTS TO PONDER

(Or the fast food version)

1. Comparison is one of Satan's main levers in manipulating our self-image: once we lose our uniqueness we have lost a part of our Christian birthright.

2. Uniqueness runs throughout the Bible. The Incarnation is unique, no other god ever made himself so vulnerable as to become a baby. And we were created in the image of this unique God.

3. The Bible is a monument to uniqueness of the individual. Four Gospels narrate the same life from four unique perspectives, aimed at four categories of reader.

4. Value-wise it becomes clear that we are equal, but not interchangeable. None of us has a full tool kit and therefore we are interdependent, each with a role to fulfil.

5. Determining the worth of a person on a relative basis is a natural consequence in a society that denies any absolute values, therefore, it may not be possible to change this, but we don't have to be caught up in the game.

6. Secular society's attempts to deal with self-image issues range from blaming dysfunctional families to searching for 'inner strength'.

7. All behaviour is motivated by something. Often our surface activities are the product of relational hurts. However, the most effective way of dealing with this relational pain is to ensure that our relationship with God is such that he is able to meet our deepest longings.

1. 2 Corinthians 10:12

2. William Barclay and E Stanley Jones for a start.

3. Most of the information in this paragraph was drawn from Selwyn Hughes' Every Day With Jesus Nov/Dec 92.

4. Isaiah 49:16

5. It is possible to teach godly behaviour rather than socially acceptable behaviour. The former teaches a child what it means to be loving in a given situation, or the need to forgive, rather than 'we don't do that'. Reasoning encourages uniqueness; without reasoning we only encourage conformity.

6. Larry Crabb, Understanding People, Marshall Pickering, page 105 'Each of us has what I like to call a Hollow Core in our personality, a central part that is empty but yearns to be filled.'

7. Bradshaw On The Family, Health Communications, Inc., page 172.

8. Page 182 Splashes of Joy, Barbara Johnson, 1992, Word Inc., Dallas, Texas. Used with permission.

9. Dr. Stephen R. Covey, Author of The Seven Habits of Highly Effective People, Simon & Schuster, New York. The quote is from a tape of the same title. Although not a Christian book, it is well worth reading.

10. This diagram and the three levels of longings have been adapted from Dr. Larry Crabb's book, Inside Out, Nav Press. The terminology and some of the definitions and parameters of various levels have been changed to illustrate a slightly different point, but the concept is Dr. Crabb's.

Chapter 7

THE ROYAL LAW

The entire law is summed up in a single command: 'Love your neighbour as yourself'. The Bible tells us to love our neighbour as ourselves on no less than ten occasions, and portrays it, along with loving God, as pivotal to all godly behaviour.[1] Some Christians wish God had expressed this in different terms because the implication that we ought to love ourselves is difficult to reconcile with their understanding. Others are quite pleased with the wording, but usually for the wrong reasons. However, we know that when a passage or passages seem confusing, the fault lies not with the passage, but with our comprehension. We also know that when something is repeated so many times, it is significant. James actually calls it the royal law.

There are three components to this statement, Love - Your neighbour - As yourself. For most of us, the ambiguity doesn't really lie with the last two, it comes with the word love. Love is one of the most ill-defined words in the English language, because it seems to encompass everything from kindness to copulating. It is of great significance to the Christian that the Greek language has several words that we translate as love, because the New Testament was written in Greek, and therefore gives a much more specific definition of what God is requiring of us.

The three main Greek words translated as love are *eros, phileo,* and *agape*. *Eros* is the root of the term erotic, which gives a clue to its definition. It is primarily a physical affinity and quite often our initial attraction. Contrary to the beliefs of some it is not something contrived by Hugh Hefner,[2] but is a part of God's over-all plan. As such, it is an extremely wholesome dynamic, but one which must be handled with caution.

Phileo is a general term which is best described as friendship love. Philadelphia, Pennsylvania is known as the city of brotherly love, because that's exactly what it means in Greek. *Phileo* love is a psychological affinity based on common values, objectives and tastes. We are the most comfortable with those with whom we have the most in common. We like people who are like us. How do you know when someone has good taste? - when it's just like yours. This is a powerful basis for friendship. *Phileo* love is, to some extent, giving our seal of approval.

Agape, on the other hand, is a self-generated love; that is, it requires nothing of the object being loved. You don't have to look the way I think you ought to look or think the way I think you ought to think - I'll love you anyway. *Agape* love is to invest one's resources in the wellbeing of another. *Agape* bestows love and respect, not because they are deserved, but because they are needed. This is exactly the way God loves us and the way he requires us to love one another.

Where the Bible links self with love, as in 'Love your neighbour as yourself', it uses *agape*. The only exceptions are such passages as 2 Timothy 3:2 which speaks of the last days when 'people will be lovers of themselves'. But the word used for this self-love, which is obviously condemned, is a derivative of *phileo*. In other words 'people pleased with themselves', or 'admiring themselves'.

The confusion enters when people treat 'love your neighbour as yourself', as though the love were phileo. This would imply an affinity towards ourselves, being pleased with ourselves or 'be as drawn towards others as you are to yourself'. Secular books do speak of loving oneself in such terms. They encourage us to be pleased with ourselves and even to be 'in love' with ourselves. The Bible doesn't use that sort of word.

An interesting comparison is Jesus' words after quoting the commands to love God and your neighbour as yourself. He said, 'All the Law and the Prophets hang on these two commandments.'[3] And when he cited 'the golden rule' (do to others what you would have them do to you) he also said, 'for this sums up the Law and the

Prophets'.[4] The fact that these two ideas both summarize the Law and the Prophets should mean there is very little difference between them. It would seem the only difference between loving your neighbour as yourself and doing for him what you would want done for yourself, is terminology. *Agape* love is not feeling, it is doing.

Following a talk on selfishness, a pastor came up to me and said, 'You say that selfishness is the opposite of love, but I have always thought it was hatred'. That actually told me more about his thinking than he supposed. He was looking at love from an affinity framework, and from that perspective he was right. However, when we consider selfishness the opposite of love it is because we are employing a commitment framework. It goes something like this:

Affinity

Love	**HATE**

Commiment

LOVE	selfishness

If to *agape* my neighbour is to invest my resources in their wellbeing, then to *agape* myself surely doesn't mean having a love affair with me. It isn't standing in front of the mirror every morning saying, 'Isn't the world lucky to have you today'. If to *agape* my neighbour is to invest in him then to *agape* myself is to make the appropriate investments in me to ensure good stewardship. Even that could sound self-centred, but I think Proverbs 19:8 helps bring it into perspective: 'He who gets wisdom loves his own soul; he who cherishes understanding prospers'. The investment in wisdom is good stewardship of the mind. Loving myself might also include denying myself such things as a second helping of pie as good stewardship of my body. I have been given stewardship responsibility for my spirit, soul, and body, but I am also to be as eager to help my neighbour with his requirements as I am with my own.

In biblical terms, self-love is simply stewardship of spirit, soul and body. Strangely enough, one of the most important psychologists in the area of self-love made such a distinction over a hundred years ago. William James wrote, 'Self-love more properly belongs under...acts, since what men mean by the name is rather a set of motor tendencies than a kind of feeling properly so called'.[5] Unfortunately, few have paid any attention to his distinctions and describe self-love as an affinity rather than an action.

RESPECT

Perhaps one of the most sought-after forms of love is respect. People don't often want handouts, but the majority do want to be respected. We are led to believe that self-respect is an integral part of being human.

From a Christian perspective self-respect could well sound as dubious as being in love with oneself, and yet several texts would seem to be referring to just that. When the world speaks of self-respect they are dealing with an entirely different entity because the only self they have to respect is their old sin nature. Until they come to Christ, they are forced to make the best of an impossible situation.

By the same token when I, as a Christian, am living as if I didn't know Christ, I find myself in an even more impossible situation regarding self-respect. Any attempt to gain self-respect in the flesh would be seeking to glorify what God has denounced and I would therefore be challenging his values. Additionally, it would mean shifting my identity to my old sin nature, which would actually undermine the foundation of my self-image. It is not possible for Christians to maintain self-respect while deliberately living out of fellowship with God. They can only kid themselves.

Real self-respect is only possible in our new nature. It is actually valuing what God is accomplishing in us. The fact that self-respect is a product of our relationship with God means that it is not relative to others around us. Paul evidently wanted to underline that fact when he wrote: 'Each one should test his own actions. Then he can take pride in himself, without comparing himself to somebody else'. [6]

Godliness still demands that we assume full responsibility for who we are, but look to God for his promised maturity. Blaming circumstances actually obstructs self-respect. On the other hand, an independent self-sufficiency displaces self-respect. It does so because self-sufficiency puts us back on the value system of the old nature, a value system we know, deep down inside, we don't respect. Only a trusting dependence on God brings us to the place where we can be fully responsible and successful and yet hope to avoid the arrogance that accompanies self-sufficiency.

Self-respect, in Christian terms, is not an achievement, it is a gift of God which is only realised as we appropriate more and more of the other gifts he has on offer. For instance, accepting responsibility for my mistakes generates self-respect, blaming others detracts from it. But it's the Bible that has convinced me of how crucial this is and the Holy Spirit who has provided the strength.

Maintaining self-respect requires a clear conscience, because in a sense it *is* a clear conscience; the two are bound up together like body and soul. They come together whether one recognises it or not. John tells us: 'If our hearts do not condemn us, we have confidence before God'. [7] Sin saps self-respect because a guilty conscience places barriers in our relationship with God who is the source of all genuine respect. It soon becomes obvious that our new identity can only be maintained by keeping a short account on sin.

This brings us quite naturally to the next chapters which

discuss dealing with setbacks. Some require acceptance and others repentance. It reminds me of the well known prayer: 'Lord give me the grace to accept the things I cannot change, the power to change the things I can, and the wisdom to know the difference'.

POINTS TO PONDER

(For those in the fast lane)

1. Love is one of the most ill-defined words in the English language, but fortunately the New Testament was written in Greek which provides a better handle.

2. When the Bible speaks of self-love, it is speaking of an objective action and not an affinity. It is not 'being pleased with myself' but 'good stewardship'.

3. Confusion is introduced when secular psychologists write of self-love which is 'being pleased with myself' and then Christians read this into the Bible.

4. Respect is one of the most sought-after forms of love. People don't often want handouts, but the majority want respect.

5. When the world speaks of self-respect they have problems, because the only self they know is the old nature, something God has condemned.

6. Self-respect is possible in my new nature because it

is actually valuing what God is doing in me. That self-respect is a product of our relationship with God and is not relative to the world around us.

7. Self-respect in Christian terms is not an achievement, it is a gift of God which develops as we appropriate the other gifts he has to offer.

8. Self-respect and a clear conscience are bound up together, because both are involved in our relationship with God.

1. Leviticus 19:18&34; Matthew 19:19,22:39; Mark 12:31&33; Luke 10:27; Romans 13:9, Galatians 5:14 (quoted above) and James 2:8.
2. The founder of Playboy Magazine and the Playboy empire, a pioneer of socially acceptable erotica.
3. Matthew 22:40   **4**. Matthew 7:12
5. William James, Psychology, Briefer Course (New York: Henry Holt, 1892) p.176
6. Galatians 6:4   **7**. 1 John 3:21

Chapter 8

RESPONSIBLE BEHAVIOUR

In addition to being a God of love, our Lord is also a God of righteousness, which places him in somewhat of a dilemma, at least by human standards. He loves sinners but cannot tolerate sin. His righteousness will not allow him to ignore it, avoid it, or hide it in the back of our sock drawer. Even forgiveness in the white light of justice, is much more complicated than one might at first imagine. 'The wages of sin is death', a principle set into motion by God, becomes something that he in his justice cannot overlook. Therefore, to forgive sin is not just a matter of overlooking an offence; it requires that the price must be paid.

The fact that God is love provides the motivation to pay this price. God solved the apparent dilemma between his love of sinners and his hatred of sin by sending his Son to pay the price. God then, in his righteousness, gave Jesus the authority to forgive sin because the price has been paid.

We will do well to remember that God's love is not merely an affinity, such as 'I love strawberries'. It is a decision to do the right thing by his fallen Creation. This is the all-time classic example of love interfacing with righteousness so perfectly that each exemplifies the character of the other: righteousness so complete that it doesn't retreat in the face of the highest possible sacrifice and love so true that it encourages the righteousness.

It is understanding the righteousness of God that lets us know that the love of God is not an airy-fairy, emotional response to mankind, but a definite, calculated, and expensive meeting of needs. This guarantees that God's love is not a pathetic flash-in-the-pan but a powerful, purposeful force that can be counted on through this life and the next.

There is another aspect to God's righteousness which directly affects us. Because in his love he has drawn us into a relationship with himself, he demands responsible behaviour on our part. The Bible is a book which, from cover to cover, demands responsibility on man's part. It is a story of God trying to get man to accept responsibility for his own actions. It starts in the Garden of Eden with Adam shifting the blame saying, 'It is that woman you gave me', and Eve saying, 'The serpent beguiled me'.

We accept Adam's and Eve's representation in plunging us into irresponsibility, just as we accept Christ's representation in paying the penalty for it. But for some, God's demand for responsible behaviour on our part seems to cast a shadow on his love. It is as though, when we think of a God of love, we think of a warm snuggly Grandfather. But this God of love wants to hold us responsible, because he is not a permissive Grandfather, he is our Father and real love is not the least bit indulgent. This love has our best interests at heart and, as such, it is long range in perspective.

We have several reasons for understanding that God has our best interests at heart. First, responsibility is a part of God's character development curriculum. He is conforming us into the image of his son. Maturity of character is not developed without assuming responsibility. In fact, the greatest sign of maturity is responsibility. The person who is not responsible is not mature.

This would definitely be out of phase with some secular treatment of self-image problems. Joanna and Alister McGrath comment in their book *The Dilemma of Self-Esteem*[1], 'The secular therapist has some difficulty with failure and adopts the somewhat defeatist attitude of lowering standards in order that everyone may succeed', Then they add, tongue in cheek, 'If at first you don't succeed, change the rules!'

For God so loved the world that he didn't move the goal posts. He doesn't lower the standards, because his objective is to raise us to meet his standards.

Secondly, we know God has our best interest at heart because all of us need this maturity. We know full well that although we do manage an acceptable level of responsibility in the major, more observable areas of life, there are gaps in our maturity. I sometimes liken maturity to an old castle. Approaching from the front the gate towers seem very formidable. A portcullis is in place. The walls are high and thick. There are turret towers with slots for bowmen and it looks like a castle should look. But when we walk around to the back we find the ravages of time have collapsed large sections. There is no protection. Here we become aware the castle is something to be photographed only from the front. A lot of us know that we are limited to a frontal view. We keep others at arm's length for fear they will go through the gate and explore far enough to find areas of construction which are way behind schedule.

UNDER CONSTRUCTION

God's concern isn't limited to a frontal view. He is building up the entire fabric of our lives. Jesus Christ didn't die so we could have a home in heaven someday, he died that we might bear the family resemblance, and not just a hollow shell or something that won't bear close scrutiny. The family resemblance is not the shell, it is the inner character. The value system of God's entire economy is in terms of character. And the character he imparts is of such a quality that it allows us to admit we don't have all the required character. It's alright to have a personality that's still under construction. We will always have to give apologies for inconveniences due to ongoing construction, but to admit this is to assume responsibility, which is a sign of maturity.

Thirdly, we know God has our best interests at heart because he does not leave us alone to carry the guilt of failure. He has not only entered us in a character development course, but he has also provided a Saviour to carry the consequences of our failure. This factor - grace - allays our fears about the lifetime character development course we find ourselves on.

Most of us don't warm to the concept of God holding us responsible, because we know that our ability to behave in a responsible manner is nothing to write home about. We don't even live up to our own standards of responsibility, let alone God's. If we assume responsibility for our own actions we will have an even lower opinion of ourselves than we do now. We will have to bear a lot of guilt.

The good news, as we have already noted, is that God's sacrifice on our behalf went far beyond securing heavenly citizenship. It deals with our guilt on a day-to-day basis. Our primary responsibility is to be obedient, but failing that the next level is to assume responsibility for our own actions. The second level of responsibility is outlined in 1 John 1:9 'If we confess our sins he is faithful and just to forgive us our sins and purify us from all unrighteousness'. Confession means to name the act and to accept full liability for our behaviour. It doesn't mean that we justify ourselves, God is prepared to do that. The degree to which we attempt to justify ourselves is the degree to which we remove ourselves from the One who freely justifies. Assuming responsibility for our behaviour is not burdensome when Jesus is willing and able to assume the guilt. Presumably this is what the Psalmist had in mind: 'Blessed be the Lord, who daily bears our burden'. [2]

BEHAVIOUR / PERFORMANCE

At this point it is necessary to introduce a crucial distinction. I am talking about behaviour and making a point of separating behaviour from performance. I am using 'performance' within the sense of skills and abilities and 'behaviour' as pertaining to rightness or wrongness of our attitudes and actions. I perform according to my skills and abilities; I behave according to my attitudes. This is not assigning special meaning to the words, it is simply restricting performance to a slightly narrower usage to avoid blurring values. I think this distinction must be made in any intelligent discussion of self-image from a Christian perspective. Secular society has no basis for making such a distinction due to a lack of an absolute standard for judging behaviour. Christians have the basis for such a distinction and need to use it to avoid blurring issues.[3]

If I perform less well than another person, that is not necessarily a sin: our abilities were not on a par to begin with. But if my behaviour falls below God's standards that is sin.

It is necessary to make this distinction for the simple reason that behaviour is never judged on a relative basis. God does not grade on a curve. I am never excused because my behaviour might be above group standards and I am never convicted by God because my behaviour falls below group standards. My behaviour is judged simply between myself and God, according to his standards.

We frequently hear comments such as, 'You're being too hard on yourself', or, 'He takes life too seriously', or, 'Don't take yourself too seriously'. Without a distinction between behaviour and performance we are ill-equipped to evaluate whether such statements could possibly be applicable in our case.

If I have a sin problem and decide that I am simply being too hard on myself, backing off won't help. I won't feel any better for 'giving myself a break' and it won't be just myself I will be taking less seriously if I do. I will be taking God less seriously, and so compounding my guilt. This, in turn, will give me all the more ammunition to hate myself. Conversely, if my problem is one of performance, where my best isn't good enough to suit me, perhaps I am 'taking myself too seriously'.

INVENTORY

We must all evaluate our gifts, abilities and assets simply to see what we are equipped for. This is simply an inventory where we identify our strengths and weaknesses. We must accept this inventory as a fact of life in order to make intelligent decisions as to what we will do in life. A jockey and a sumo wrestler can't hope to trade places. Height, looks, aptitudes and abilities are the tools involved as we develop our performance. They were all provided by a sovereign God to equip us for our part in his plan. This is the part we accept and come to grips with, the performance factors. However, to talk about self-acceptance with no distinction in terms is often meant and interpreted as accepting behaviour problems as well, forgetting that behaviour has a moral component. To accept the fact that I am a head taller than most, or that I can't carry a tune, is maturity. To accept being a liar or an adulterer is to throw God's salvation back in his face.

The blurring of these distinctions between behaviour and performance frequently creates problems in helping people with a poor self-image. Counsellors who fail to make this distinction could find themselves encouraging behaviour problems which actually need to be corrected. Often this is because their world view lumps most of human activity into the performance area. For instance, one secular counselling book suggests:

> As a helper, you can do a great deal to help people develop a sense of agency or self-efficacy. First, you can help them challenge self-defeating beliefs and attitudes about themselves and substitute realistic beliefs about self-efficacy.[4]

The 'self-defeating beliefs and attitudes', referred to above, in a world without moral and ethical absolutes could 'cover a multitude of sins'. From a secular perspective a behaviour is only a sin if it adversely affects someone else. If a person feels bad about themselves, you simply help him find what he does well and encourage him in it. 'So you have a slight fixation on pornography John, you're still one of our best teachers.'

Jay Adams has a very direct method of ensuring that behaviour that needs to be corrected is not encouraged. To a client who claims to be worthless he would say:

> You probably have some good reasons for having reached that conclusion about yourself. Tell me about them.[5]

By pursuing his client's own evaluation Dr. Adams may be helping them face their responsibility. It is a question any of us would do well to ask ourselves when we feel worthless.

However, feelings of worthlessness aren't always the result of sinful behaviour, they may be associated with our performance. Some Christian counsellors would have difficulty with that because they see low self-image as almost entirely the result of sin.

Jay Adams, for example quotes a survey of some 200 criminals and concludes that none of them had a self-image problem because, 'each criminal thought of himself as a basically good person...even when planning a crime'.[6] That is basically saying there are no self-image problems without guilt. I believe there is a significant number of people who feel worthless with no reason to feel guilty, because their problems are not behaviour - but performance-related. But, it is necessary to separate the two. We will be considering performance in the next chapter.

PERSONAL HOPE AND RECONSTRUCTION

The fact that a person may have things pretty well nailed down in the observable areas of life does not mean he or she is a superior person. They are still under construction. Conversely, the fact that one of the areas which is still under construction is out front for all to see, does not make them inferior.

A ministry colleague, Gordon Westbrook, who has now graduated, was a truly wonderful gentleman. He was very sensitive, loving, considerate, soft-spoken, easy to get along with. It often seemed to me that he was everything I wasn't. My goal-oriented temperament brings with it a great tendency to be aggressive and insensitive. It is one of many areas of my life that is still under construction. It was quite natural for me to wish I was more like Gordon. However, I had no business feeling inferior to him because he was having victories in areas where I was still having defeats. I needed simply to be thankful for the example that God had provided through his life. Conversely, Gordon would have had no right to feel superior to me because he was having

111

victories in areas where I was having defeats.

Righteousness is not relative. Behaviour cannot be judged on a curve. Sin has a lot of adverse effects in my life but it does not make me inferior to other sinners and that is all I have to compare with in this world. Consequently, I must avoid comparison with any human for value judgments, because Paul tells us when we measure ourselves by ourselves we are not wise.

The object of this exercise is not to make anyone comfortable with their sin, because we are also foolish if we do not continually aim for God's standards. The object is to bring us to the point where we can say: 'I can't afford to lose hope just because there are so many "spiritual heavy-weights" who obviously have everything so well glued together, when I am still under construction'.

POINTS TO PONDER

(Even in the bath tub)

1. The object of the Incarnation and Crucifixion was not so much to get us all up to heaven as to make us like Jesus.

2. Since this is God's over-all objective he is much more committed to our maturity than he is to our personal comfort.

3. It also means that another way in which God's love

is manifested towards us is in holding us responsible for our behaviour.

4. The good news is that he offers us a second level of responsibility. If we fail to be responsible in obedience, he will still restore us if we will assume responsibility for our sinful behaviour. (To confess a wrong means to assume responsibility for it.)

5. It is important in examining our shortcomings that we make a distinction between behaviour and performance. The former has to do with the rightness or wrongness of our actions and the latter with our skills and abilities. This is important because we respond to them differently.

6. I can accept the fact that I am a head taller than most or that I can't carry a tune, but to accept being a liar or an adulterer is to throw God's gift back in his face.

7. I can't accept sin in my life, but by the same token, I can accept that it is alright to be under construction.

1. The Dilemma of Self-Esteem Joanna and Alister McGrath, Crossway Books, Wheaton and Cambridge
2. Psalm 68:19 NASB
3. I recognize that there are times when performance and behaviour seem to overlap, because of their interaction, but even then careful discernment can separate the two. For instance, if I am too lazy to prepare for an examination or a sermon, it will impair my performance. My poor performance is then actually a behaviour problem.
4. The Skilled Helper Gerard Egan, Brooks/Cole Publishing p. 14
5. The Biblical View of Self-Esteem, Self-Love, Self-Image Jay Adams, Harvest House p. 98
6. Ibid page 99. [Yochelson and Samenow, at St. Elizabeth's Hospital]

Chapter 9

PERFORMANCE

I am certainly aware that God's love gives me a value far beyond anything I can understand, and through his righteousness he has taught me to be responsible to him, regardless of what is going on around me. However, I am still competing in a very real world. Although my behaviour should not be measured on a relative basis within society, my performance certainly is. For instance, my employer evidently values me according to my very modest pay packet; the local football club values me only as a stand-in; and the church allows me to pass out hymn books. My performance is definitely measured on a relative basis with real people in a real world and I feel very insignificant.

It seems to me that my spiritual relationship with God in the vertical dimension somehow doesn't quite touch the horizontal world I live in - at least not as practically as I would like. I am in 'the real world', in competition with real people, some of whom are Christians, but most of whom are not. I find little evidence that the value God places on me helps with promotions or pay rises, causes me to be accepted into society (even Christian society) or allows me to do anything of significance.

114

If I spoke like this with any of my Christian friends I would receive any number of spiritual 'potions'. I would receive advice all the way from claiming my inheritance to the fact that I am not really looking to God.

I have actually become comfortable enough in my vertical relationship with God that my whole idea of significance is to serve him. But from my limited perspective, I still don't see this vertical relationship giving me the necessary 'street credibility' to allow effective input to my world. I can't help believing that advancement in any area would increase my effectiveness.

A lot of people could probably identify with the preceding paragraphs; it is not the least bit strange to see things this way. Nevertheless, it is based on a failure to comprehend the sovereignty of God, and that's definitely the crucial factor concerning performance.

Performance can be measured by relative standards and it is not wrong to do so. This is why it is important to make a sharp distinction between performance and behaviour. It would seem ridiculous to conclude that an athlete crosses the finish line first on any other basis than superior performance. The winner may not be the best runner overall, but on that day, in that race his or her performance was definitely superior. Perhaps the person in last place (with the most inferior performance) pulled a muscle, and would otherwise have been yards ahead of the winner. But the fact is, the winner's performance on that given day was superior to all others and could be measured and recorded. This is a fact of life and so much so that it is used as an example by Paul in his letters.[1]

There are several categories of truth: there are facts which can be scientifically proven, those which can be historically verified, and those of the Bible. Science is sometimes faulty and even when we get good solid facts, society frequently misses the implications because it lacks a biblical overview. Consequently, almost everything in life is measured in some way and compared on a relative basis and this, supposedly, is its value.

Any performance can be measured and compared, if not in dramatic terms like a race, then it can be scored as in diving or figure skating. Preaching can be rated on speaking ability, the significance and arrangement of material presented, and the preacher's ability to hold our attention. We will have to admit that this is largely entertainment value. The real value of a sermon is not in the performance, but in the way God uses it in the hearts of those who hear it.

Performance cannot be ignored, but that is not the value of the message or the person giving it. Many of us have enjoyed logical, well-polished sermons delivered by speakers with great dexterity in the Word. At the same time we frequently have to admit that these same sermons had little impact on our lives. On the other hand, I personally have been pricked to the heart and challenged to action by messages that were delivered poorly and not at all well organised.

This is not an excuse for sloppy craftsmanship; we have a responsibility to do the best we can 'as unto the Lord'. This goes for anything we do, whether it be repairing a boiler, or leading a large international ministry. Anything less is a behaviour problem. It is sin and needs to be dealt with as such.

I work hard putting talks together but when I stand up to give them I am no longer relying on the fact that I have done my homework to bring value to the message. Because I know that God is not relying on my ability, but my availability, it relieves me of the pressure to perform.

If the talk appears unsuccessful, I must evaluate my part. The source of the trouble may not have actually been a performance problem, it may have been that I was relying on my ability to perform and God wanted to teach me a lesson, or I may have been too lazy to put in the necessary work. I call these behavioural problems because they can be separated from ability. They are sinful heart attitudes which affect my performance but they have nothing to do with my actual ability to perform.

GOD DETERMINES SUCCESS.

But if, after I have searched my heart, I find I have a clear conscience, I cannot allow myself to feel inferior, for two reasons. First, success is God's business, not mine. He did not call me to be apparently successful, only to be available. Secondly, he is sovereign and he alone determines success. He may be aware of seeds planted in many hearts that will not bear fruit in my lifetime; they may not even begin to sprout while I'm alive.

Let me tell you about Johnny Boatwater. When we met him, he was a senior non-commissioned officer in the U.S. Air Force. He and his wife Camellia are two of the sweetest Christians you would ever want to meet. Johnny was stationed in Thailand during the Vietnam war for a number of years. Normally the tour is only 15 months but Johnny got so tied up in events that he kept extending. Their marriage was already a mess before he was assigned to Thailand so it was no motivation to return home. Johnny took advantage of the cheap booze and then got involved in drugs.

He also got involved in Buddhism to the extent that he became a Buddhist priest. He went through some extremely bizarre initiation rights where his arms were stabbed with long needles and knives without him feeling a thing (and he was sober). He was also slashed across the back with a sword, which made his friend who came to witness the rite, scream out. It bled, but Johnny didn't feel it and it had miraculously healed a day later leaving no scar. They tattooed Johnny around the neck and over his shoulders and various other places. The symbols were easily recognized and feared by the local Thai residents. This was an elite cult.

Johnny had developed a tremendous capacity for alcohol, drinking at least two bottles of spirits a day. When he finally did leave Thailand he was stationed at Greenham Common, in England. What cheap booze there was, was rationed and Johnny hadn't yet identified a really reliable drug source.

Two cleaning women in the NCO barracks could see he was at a crisis point in his life and began praying for him. They witnessed to him one day to which he responded by wrenching the Buddha from inside his shirt and telling them he didn't need their Jesus because he had Buddha, a more powerful god. They still kept on praying even though they gave him a little more space.

The crunch came the day after Christmas. Johnny hadn't monitored his booze supply very well and hadn't been able to get hold of a drink for a critically long time. The cleaning women came up to the barracks with some Christmas goodies just as Johnny ventured out of his room like a bear out of its cave. He stared at the women who could see his desperate condition and trembled within. This probably only lasted a few seconds although it seemed much longer. Then for no apparent reason Johnny went over to them, dropped down on his knees and threw his arms around the legs of one of them, sobbing for Jesus. The women's husbands were just downstairs and the four of them went back into Johnny's room to pray and counsel him into the family of God.

Johnny went on from strength to strength. He is immediately recognized as a leader in the black Christian military wherever he goes. His wife soon followed his conversion and together they have shepherded and nurtured hundreds of young servicemen and women. As we know, it wasn't the polished performance of a great evangelist that the Lord used to bring Johnny through, it was the faithfulness of two cleaning women. Their performance probably was not too impressive, but God uses what we faithfully provide. When the picture is all completed and credit is given, these two women will not only be rewarded for their own faithfulness, but they will share in the glory of all God has done through Johnny and Camellia.

The fact of God giving value to the performance holds true even in the secular world where people are hired and fired on their ability to perform. It could be that the man with the poorest performance on the staff (provided his behaviour is right) is making the greatest impact for God. One may well ask, 'How can this be when he is not respected for his performance?' The fact is that even secular man knows deep down inside that there is more to life than performance. Integrity is admired, if only in secret, even in a 'dog eat dog' world, because it is a vanishing quality. It may well be when all attempts to improve performance fail, that it is a signal to change career fields. And sometimes God supernaturally augments our performance to bring success in order to enhance our witness. However, I wouldn't bank much on the latter, because God seems to delight in making the greatest mileage from the smallest amount of apparent success.

The baseline fact is that the value of a person does not rest on his ability to sell cars, type like a machine gun, or programme computers; nor is his eternal significance determined by a large, apparently successful, ministry. People who have so-called 'full-time' Christian occupations are not more significant in God's economy than a bricklayer or a book-keeper who is under the Lordship of Christ. I'm a firm believer in sanctified secular employment. If God calls me to be a book-keeper, then I must be God's book-keeper. I will be the best book-keeper I can and at the same time attempt to bring every asset under my control to the glory of God.

I may have many apparently 'spiritual' opportunities in my journey or I may have few, but I do not want any of them to fail because I was not faithful in my basic calling. I know that the few I do have can be just as eternally significant as the pastor's many. The fact is that all of our life is one long spiritual opportunity, if for no other reason than that people are reading the message of it. There are frequently more people reading the lives of lay people than that of their pastors.

I cannot determine the value of my own performance any more than I can determine the number of oranges in an orange seed or apples in an apple seed. When one attempts to estimate the yield from one seed there are too many factors to consider. Will it even take root, or will it simply rot in the ground? How large will the new plant grow? How much fruit will it bear? And last of all, how many of those seeds will be planted in turn?

POINTS TO PONDER

(But not enough to give you a headache)

1. Unlike my behaviour, my performance can be measured on a relative basis, i.e. it can be compared with the performance of others.

2. Therefore, in spite of my relationship with the God who loves me, I may still feel insignificant.

3. So I need to have the biblical perspective on my performance, namely that God is sovereign over it.

4. God determines the value and significance of my performance on any given occasion.

5. The important thing is that I make my every skill and

Chapter 10

THE CENTRE

Some writers use the term *other-centredness* as the opposite of self-centredness and, in a sense, I suppose it is. We certainly understand what they are saying, but using other-centredness as an antonym for self-centredness presents problems in a Christian context. To say I am self-centred means that self is the central focus of my life, the very core around which I orbit. The analogy of having a 'centre' breaks down the moment we introduce more than one centre. To speak of changing from self-centredness to other-centredness is certainly honourable and I'm relatively sure most Christians who speak of the need to be other-centred would also assume Christ-centredness even though their terminology actually precludes it.

Self-centredness can only be successfully overcome through Christ-centredness. Etiquette and good manners are society's attempt to remove the abrasive edge from human selfishness. Encouraging someone through the door ahead of us or giving them first choice of teacakes is a social attempt at other-centredness. But social graces such as courtesy, politeness or even chivalry are only hollow caricatures of real selflessness. Other people simply don't have the magnetism for us to break away from our own self-centred field of gravity - at least not long enough for it to be taken seriously as other-centredness. Only God can provide the necessary force for us to break loose from self into a new orbit around Jesus Christ.

The fact of being Christ-centred provides us the power to be other-oriented, but we cannot be other-centred. We can only orbit around one centre at a time. Concern for others is simply not enough to attract us out of orbit around ourselves, only Christ centredness can free us to be other-oriented. One can only be self-centred or Christ-centred. Being Christ-centred means to please the Lord rather than ourselves. Pleasing the Lord provides us a pure motive for being other-oriented.

TECHNIQUE OR CHARACTER?

Certainly, some unregenerate humans are successful at relationships, proving they have been successful at a measure of other-orientedness. This does not, however, mean they are selfless. Self-centredness uses a type of other-orientedness as a technique to serve self, Christ-centredness uses other-orientedness to serve the Lord who has their (as well as our) best interests at heart. Using other-orientedness as an interpersonal relationship technique is more of a skill based on understanding human needs, social expectations and other talents used in lubricating human interaction. It also involves a long range focus, self-discipline and some help from our temperament. But even those favoured with a temperament conducive to decorum, a long range focus and bags of self-discipline, can easily be pushed to their limit. When our underlying motivation is self-centredness there comes a time when the investment in others proves too unprofitable.

Unfortunately, just as an unbeliever can develop other-orientedness as a technique, so a Christian can be totally self-centred. It would be nice if becoming a Christian automatically made us Christ-centred, if one decision covered everything and we could live a sinless life. The best we can do is to decide that we will make all future decisions in favour of Christ, but that still leaves us with billions of opportunities to go back on that original decision, which we all, unfortunately, do from time to time. Spiritual growth could be defined simply as going back on our original commitment less frequently.

Most of us recognize our human inadequacies when it comes to front line ministries like teaching a Sunday school class or witnessing to others, and we become totally reliant on God. However, in day-to-day living we tend to make such a decision only when we fully understand what absolute failures we are and how much we require his grace. So-called 'front line' ministries and day-to-day living are really no different. Joyce and I have been teaching Christian marriage relationship principles for so long we could do it in our sleep. The fact that we may be skilled and knowledgable in this area should allow us to perform well, but if our efforts are to have eternal impact we must be relying on the Holy Spirit and not our performance.

A POLITE TEMPERAMENT?

It is in the area of day-to-day living where those blessed with a suitable temperament and up-bringing may well be disadvantaged. They are and always have been 'nice people'. It comes naturally to them, just as teaching does to me, and I have to make a conscious effort to remember, in Christ's words, 'By myself, I can do nothing'. On the other hand, I am not a skilled 'liver'. My goal oriented temperament tends to reduce any social graces I have acquired to mere protocol which has to be memorized and reviewed for special occasions. The advantage of this is not exactly a bragging point - I know I am a self-centred klutz. My prayer life is equally self-centred - I spend most of my prayer time apologizing for what I do when not praying and then for not praying enough.

In a recent counselling session I found myself having great difficulty maintaining a Christian, or even a professional attitude as the husband continued to hark back to his 'underprivileged' childhood. Another counsellor had helped him to rediscover his childhood and the pain in his soul as the reason for much of his current behaviour. He was insensitive, arrogant, judgemental and so self-centred that the slightest discomfort was unthinkable. He seemed to believe forgiving others was only required of those whose childhood was too smooth to authorize bitterness. In his view, confession and repentance were unnecessary if a reason for the sin could be identified, and the fact that he was one of the few selected to continually suffer the discomforts of life, was reason enough.

I had an easier time maintaining my patience once I realized the reason I had taken such an immediate dislike to this guy was that he reminded me too much of myself! He was demonstrating the very things I can't stand about myself, because I would like to think I have grown out of these traits, but I know they are there just below the surface.

ETIQUETTE AS A WEAPON

Just last month I caught myself being polite, hoping to embarrass some dinner guests. The couple were short on manners and when Joyce served the dessert, they dived right in not waiting for their hostess to be seated. My mother-in-law and I just sat there waiting for Joyce to be seated. I don't know what my mother-in-law was thinking, but I was hoping they would notice they were the only ones stuffing their faces and realize what clods they were. They didn't, but I certainly realised my motives were about as far from Christian love as they could get. It certainly brought home Jeremiah 17:9 with a thump. 'The heart is deceitful above all things and beyond cure. Who can understand it?'

It is these revelations that help me to realise that my only hope is to throw myself on the mercy of God and scoop up all the grace he will allow. A ministry that is not Christ-centred can have no eternal impact and an individual life cannot please the Lord if it is not totally dependant upon him.

I can intellectually accept the premise that Jesus Christ is the indispensable core of significant personal effectiveness, but somehow it is not until I see myself as a worthless slob that I am actually ready to fall at his feet and appropriate all that he is into all that I'm not. Only then do I actually experience the power of my relationship with him. The reason is that 'admitting' our need for Jesus has become a natural part of evangelical vocabulary. But when it comes to the really significant measurement - human character - admitting I'm both immature and irresponsible hits much closer to home.

All of a sudden I'm no longer just one of a congregation, I am the one without a passing grade in Life 101. This gets my attention and it's embarrassing, but it should be cause for celebration because now I'm finally ready to do something about it. Before, I could sit back with the rest of my fellow evangelicals in comfortable anonymity, admitting I need Jesus. Now everything depends on whether or not he will bail me out.

And just what is the key that will ensure that Jesus will bail me out? Harking back to Roy Hession, 'The only way to acquire grace is to admit you need it'. By this time I'm ready to admit I need his grace. The really exciting thing at this point (that I may not even recognize) is that I have finally come to an end of myself: I have come face to face with the fact that my resources are inadequate for effective day-to-day living. This alone will ensure Christ-centredness, which will in turn ensure other-orientedness and the only positive cure for my basic selfishness. Effective day-to-day living is now possible in a way never before considered possible.

FOUNDATIONS

It may also be helpful to talk about foundations. At first glance there may not seem to be a lot of difference between foundations and centres, but a slight change in analogies sometimes provides alternative perspectives. There are different foundations upon which it is possible to build our identities. These foundations are in fact values and I actually become the values I build on. The insidious thing is that we are not always becoming the values we have intellectually accepted. Often we are unwittingly building on society's values and thereby becoming more a reflection of society than of Christ. Why do young people outgrow their faith? If they do, it is because they have fallen into the trap of building their identity upon the same secular values as their friends. Many haven't actually outgrown their faith, they just simply wouldn't know who they were if they embraced it more closely.

Many of the possible foundations for building our identity fall in the general category of achievement. This is very popular because we like things under our control, so if we are the least bit gifted, building our self-image on achievement suits us down to the ground. We may be into athletics, art, scholarship or just plain making money. The fact is that even if our achievements are entirely intrinsically motivated, we secretly hope they will turn a profit one day. But whether making money has anything to do with it or not, it is an identity based on ability - I am what I can do, and being a pro means I can really do it well!

Another type of foundation is *relational*. It is an identity based on belonging, on being accepted and respected by others. This is a very predictable consequence of our need to relate. We were created to be relational beings, in the image of God who is, himself, a relational being. The fact that we are strongly motivated to relate is a result of creation. The fact that we have difficulty relating is a result of the fall. Basing our self-image on our human attachments is yet another result of the fall. When Paul wrote: 'I laid a foundation as an expert builder',[1] he was talking about the entire 'package' of information that we call the Gospel. It was the truth that fills up the Hollow Core, that influences all that we do and are. We are not to build anything (certainly not our identity) on any other foundation: 'For no one can lay any foundation other than the one already laid, which is Jesus Christ'.[2]

Achievement foundations are saying, 'I am what I can do'. Relational foundations are saying, 'I am what others think of me'. Building our identity on Jesus

Christ is saying, 'I am God's man/woman and to some degree an extension of his character and a channel of his love' (because he is developing the character of Christ in my life, which includes loving through me).

Joanna and Alister McGrath speak of four *domains* from which we draw our self-esteem: pedigree, the love of another, the performance of roles (which is mainly achievement), and eternal significance. They then proceed to tie all of them into attachment and avoidance of separation.

Pedigree is obviously related to parental and family bonds.

The love of another is attachment by another name.

The performance of roles is one way the love of another can be earned or maintained, leading to attachment and the avoidance of separation.

Eternal significance is clearly a way in which death, the final separation, can be repudiated. By passing something of oneself onto people left behind, the impression of permanent attachment is created.

They then go on to comment, 'The survival value of attachment behaviour is beyond dispute. But for the Christian, it is of deep interest and potential richness. In that the creation mirrors its creator, however imperfectly, we can expect that human relationships may point to aspects of our relationship to God'.[3] It would seem they are saying that what psychologists term attachment behaviour, is actually reflecting the fact that God intended relationship to be the foundation of our identity, but it was to be our relationship with him!

The fact is that the foundation of our self-image becomes the engine of our life - the supreme driving force.

Therefore, it isn't sufficient to say we are Christ-centred. That may be what we hope to be or want to be. We have to ask ourselves, 'What is the engine of my life? Am I powered by the driving force of achievement? Or is the fear of separation or rejection the motivating force in my life?'

> Fear of man will prove to be a snare, but whoever trusts in the Lord is kept safe.[4]

The sixth chapter of Romans provides the hope of being driven by the right force because it is my old self that is concerned with achievement and which fears man: 'For we know that our old self was crucified with him so that the body of sin might be rendered powerless, that we should no longer be slaves to sin'. That is, verse six lets me know I can be 'disconnected' from the wrong driving force, and verse eighteen 'connects' me to the right one. 'You have been set free from sin and have become slaves to righteousness.'

Dying to self is not crucifying our personalty, gifts or abilities. It is dying to the independent spirit which has been the motivational force behind them. Who is in the driver's seat, my old independent spirit, which is sin, or God's Holy Spirit resident in me? Under the control of the Holy Spirit, my personality and the use of my abilities will come across differently, it will still be me - but the new me. The new me is the real me that has been redeemed. God redeemed the person - mind, emotion, will, body, personality, abilities - all that go together to make me. All of that he redeemed, but not the sinful nature.

It isn't that a person can't accomplish great things without the Lord. God has given us wonderful abilities such as inventing, writing, and creating things of beauty. But great accomplishments can still leave us feeling hollow and unfulfilled. We often find, when reading the lives of people of great achievement, that they ended tragically. We certainly can't achieve anything of eternal significance, apart from God.

God never meant me to identify with my old nature because it was not part of his original creation of man. The frailty of my old nature and all the forces it has been vulnerable to have been the driving force of my life. But when I am redeemed, I have been bought from that old nature and given a new nature which is meant to be the driving force. Paul said, 'I die every day'[5] which is surely a powerful way of acknowledging the death of the old and living in the control of the new.

Establishing that the right person is in control leads next to refining our objectives.

POINTS TO PONDER

(Fast food for thought)

1. Other people simply don't have the magnetism for us to break away from our own self-centred field of gravity - at least not long enough for it to be taken seriously as other-centredness.

2. Only God can provide the necessary force for us to break loose from self into a new orbit around Jesus Christ.

3. Self-centredness uses a type of other-orientedness as a technique to serve self, Christ-centredness uses other-orientedness to serve the Lord who has their (as well as our) best interests at heart.

4. We are not always becoming the values we have intellectually accepted, we may unwittingly be building on society's values and thereby becoming more a reflection of society than of Christ.

5. Our self-image may be built on a foundation of achievement or it may be on a relational foundation, what others think of us. But it is certain that whatever is the foundation of our self-image will become the driving force of our life.

1. I Corinthians 3:10   **2**. I Corinthians 3:11
3. Joanna and Alister McGrath, The Dilemma of Self-Esteem (Crossway Books, Wheaton and Cambridge 1992) p. 64.
4. Proverbs 29:25   **5**. I Corinthians 15:31

Chapter 11

ARE YOU TROUBLED BY TROUBLE?[1]

Jesus said, 'Do not let your hearts be troubled',[2] not long before he said, 'In this world you will have trouble'.[3] The combination of these two verses reveals a very crucial truth.

In this world, trouble is inevitable - being troubled is optional. Jesus wouldn't have said, 'Do not <u>let</u> your hearts be troubled', unless we had a choice. He made it perfectly clear that he wasn't providing us with any supernatural powers to avoid trouble, but being in trouble and being troubled are two different things.

Ever feel that life is composed of problems? There have certainly been times in my life when there seemed to be very little space between them, and frequently an awful lot of overlap. Some people believe that without problems life would lose its zest. Most of us enjoy a certain amount of challenge and we frequently recognize God's hand in developing maturity in the problems he allows.

However, we also recognize that some of our problems are no more than self-inflicted wounds: we have actually 'shot ourselves in the foot'. Our own selfishness has caused us to be less sensitive to others than we should have been, and now we are paying the price. We may have been a bit too aggressive in the way we handled a client and now his nose is out of joint. And how many times have we heard, 'When am I going to learn to keep my big mouth shut?' Proverbs speaks of the cause-and-effect nature of observing the rules of life: 'For as churning the milk produces butter, and as twisting the nose produces blood, so stirring up anger produces strife'.[4] In other words there is no effect without a cause.

HOW MANY HAVE SELF-IMAGE PROBLEMS?

What has being troubled by trouble to do with self-image? It is simply that a goodly number of such self-inflicted wounds are directly traceable to a self-image problem. I am <u>not</u> saying 'At the root of every human problem is a self-image problem', mainly because the bottom line is actually attempting to live life independent of God. However, since independence from God distorts our perception of the world and everything in it, it is not surprising that it would distort our self-image and contribute to the impression that our root problem is a poor self-image. <u>The root problem is independence from God.</u> This is why it is not possible to solve human problems apart from God.

This self-image manifestation of our independence touches more areas than many expect. I have no quotable sources on the percentage of people with self-image problems, although I have heard figures cited as high as 99% of the population being affected to some degree. However, I don't really need a figure from some eminent researcher to tell you that estimate is off by exactly one per cent. Looking at this Christianly, I believe it would be inconsistent with sound doctrine to believe that all of us are not either afflicted, have been healed or are being healed of this problem.

I base this assertion on such statements as, 'We all, like sheep, have gone astray, each of us has turned to his own way'[5] and, 'there is no-one who understands, no-one who seeks God',[6] and several similar passages. We were made to function in relationship with God. Anything less is hazardous to our well-being and detracts from our potential as image-bearers. Our sense of significance and security were meant to come from him.

Even as committed Christians, the lapses where we look to other mortals and 'things' to satisfy us are often more than momentary. Consequently, we have all suffered the trauma of our own sinful independence and the resultant scar tissue has, to some degree, distorted the way we view ourselves. A healthy self-image is not possible apart from the Creator.

COMPENSATING BEHAVIOUR

How do most of us deal with our feelings of inadequacy? Do we recognize they are the result of attempting to function independently of God and do we repent of our independence? Most of us are too thick to recognize what is happening and possibly too stiff-necked to repent when we do become aware.

There is quite an inventory of compensating behaviour associated with a poor self-image. Just as I was completing this book I came across an article in a counselling journal by John Sturt that outlined some major types of behaviour people unconsciously use to compensate for feelings of inadequacy.[7] Here is his list of possible symptoms or compensating behaviours and his list of possible long term results or prognoses.

Compensating Behaviours:
1. Excessive shyness
2. Draw attention to yourself
3. Put yourself down
4. Boasting, bragging and exaggeration
5. Dogmatism
6. Suspicion and criticism
7. Rigid thinking
8. Aggression
9. Workaholism

His catalogue of Long Term Results included the following, not all of which are necessarily long range, but none the less they are definitely results and not compensating behaviours.

Long Term Results:
1. **Jealousy**
2. **Anger**
3. **Guilt**
4. **Stress**
5. **Intimacy Failure**
6. **Loneliness**
7. **Depression**
8. **Distorted picture of God**

These are pretty well recognised consequences of stress. Richard Ecker states, 'If you have a problem with unwanted stress, you have a problem with your self-concept'.[8]

Having a self-image problem is often the last thing a person with a poor self-image is willing to own up to. The above has been reproduced in the hope that a few may recognize the source of some of their problems. Discovering that some of our problems are in fact self-inflicted wounds doesn't actually boost the ego, but it is the first step towards a 'damage containment' strategy and on to healing. I see so many people suffering from problems in this area who wouldn't even consider that the way they viewed themselves was contributing to their injury. This is not limited to spiritual pygmies, I know some real spiritual 'heavy weights' who would recognize themselves on one or both of these lists if they were honest. When a person refuses to acknowledge any self-image impairment whatsoever, they forfeit a valuable tool in evaluating their motives.

WHAT CONSTITUTES A PROBLEM?

Any time we find we are repeatedly doing things we wish we wouldn't, we have a problem. Such problem behaviour can range from nail biting to wife beating and they may vary in frequency. Under the rationale 'no-one is perfect', we learn to live with a bit of nail biting, but there is a limit to anything. If we are to move forward as believers or just simply as human beings, we must deal with any of our personal behaviour which might be hurtful to others and even that which is merely restricting our own human potential.

There is no effect without a cause. Why is it that some people can handle so much more 'trouble' than others? Why do some take it in their stride while others seem to fall apart? Those of us who lack a good childhood foundation have the additional burden of dealing with that poor foundation. Even those we consider to be secure in Christ are occasionally caught out in an 'old nature knee jerk reaction'. Paul makes it clear that our old man is crucified.

> For we know that our old self was crucified with
> him so that the body of sin might be done away
> with, that we should no longer be slaves to sin.[9]

Yet under pressure, even those secure in Christ can be tricked into dragging the old nature out for a breath of fresh air. The result is at best a lack of continuity in our spiritual walk, or a real 'falling apart'. If this is true for a mature Christian, how much more so for one who is just coming to grips with his inaccurate self-image.

RESENTMENT CAN BE A LIFE STRATEGY

One thing I would add to Dr. Sturt's list of Long Term Results is bitterness. Some people live with the bitterness that comes from failure to forgive those they hold primarily responsible for lowering their self-worth: usually this is our father, mother (or both); perhaps siblings, peers, teachers and even spouses. This is definitely damaging.

As we have seen, some insecure people are dogmatic, suspicious, critical and rigid thinkers. For some these strategies form a first line of defence against possible criticism of their own conduct. Along with their own suspicions and criticisms of others, they also have on file any derogatory material that tends to back up their opinions. Forgiveness would require them to destroy these 'unfavourable information folders', an act that would leave them feeling very vulnerable indeed. Their relational security has been in having something to 'hold against' those individuals who might pose a threat to them.

Another category of individual who suffers bitterness associated with poor self-image is the person who feels so wounded that their pain becomes a life dominating force. To them the hurt is so large it is inescapable.

MEN AND WOMEN DEAL WITH THINGS DIFFERENTLY

It is fairly well accepted that women, by and large, are more willing to bring their emotions to the surface to examine and hopefully deal with them. Men, on the other hand, are not as willing to do this; they would be much more apt to bury difficult feelings and get on with trying to be somebody. This is possibly the reason many believe poor self-image is mainly a woman's problem which is, of course, far from the truth.

The fact of women being so much more on speaking terms with their emotions may well mean that they are in greater jeopardy of becoming victims of them. She may run the risk of being overcome by bitterness. This is not to say a man in the same situation will have dealt any more effectively with his hurt. The fact that he has ignored or buried an offence certainly doesn't mean he has forgiven the offender.

Failure to forgive, whether one has buried the offence or is still visibly hurt by it, still blocks the road to a healthy self-image for two reasons. First, it is sin, and sin takes us out of fellowship with the only one who can bring real value to our life. Secondly, it damages us for as long as we hold on to it; the only way to really set an offence aside is to forgive it.

The result of this male/female difference in dealing with unforgiveness is that men, being less 'in touch' with their feelings will often take some convincing that they have not actually dealt properly with a particular hurt. Women, on the other hand, are much more apt to recognize their unforgiveness, but may be so overwhelmed by the hurt that they feel unable to do anything about it. These are generalities, but can add helpful insight.

Life isn't ruined by the sins committed against us, but by the way we respond to those sins. Fortunately, as forgiveness is something God demands, it is something for which God provides the strength. That's one of the great things about God's Word: we know that any time God commands something he also makes it possible. He is a righteous and just God and would not command anything beyond our control.

Forgiveness is a decision, not an emotion. This decision is about a commitment never to bring up the offence again to the offender, to others or to ourselves. Forgiveness is separating the sin from the sinner. Forgiveness

143

is seldom easy, and is not without cost. We have to relinquish our right to get even.

FORGIVENESS IS UNFAIR

There is nothing fair about forgiveness. Forgiveness isn't fair, it's gracious - and grace is something we don't deserve. We don't forgive someone who hurts us because they deserve it, but because it is necessary to maintain fellowship with the only One who could possibly forgive all our sins when *we* didn't deserve to be forgiven for any.

It may be this unfairness that makes it difficult for some to keep an offence set aside. Maintaining an attitude of forgiveness often takes more effort than forgiving in the first place. We can easily negate the forgiveness so painstakingly acquired by simply allowing ourselves to take it up again through self-pity. The other person may be completely unaware that we are holding something against them, but we know it because we have completely lost our peace again. Self-pity is destructive even when it seems to be justified. Therefore, it is one of Satan's favourite tools.

One way to say 'no' to self-pity is to begin praying for the offending party. We can pray for ourselves while we are at it. Prayer is necessary in this commitment, such as: 'Lord I thank you that you are in control of this situation. Please continue to strengthen me in this commitment and please bless John as he works through his own feelings in the situation.' Forgiveness is a matter of renewing the mind. Exactly the same attitude file skills discussed in chapters 4 and 5 are required in forgiveness. It is not kidding ourselves that we have forgotten the offence, but rather making a deliberate entry in our attitude file of our commitment to release the offender. We stand a better chance of being able to genuinely forget the offence if we exercise this bit of mental discipline than if we don't. Healing of pain doesn't come from hiding it.

SETBACKS NEED NOT BE DEFEAT

In the latter years of her life my mother and I grew farther and farther apart philosophically.   Although she maintained a number of 'traditional values', I think she thought I was a religious prude. She would say, 'I have my life to live and you have yours', but she seemed always on the lookout for cracks in my Christianity. And she was successful. I would lose my 'Kingdom Living' with predictable regularity. I would like to think I had grown past that now but I know that if she were alive today, she would still find cracks now and then. That doesn't mean I haven't forgiven her for various childhood hurts, or that I am holding things against her, but all of us find that current clashes call up old pains which can still knock us off balance. They need to be dealt with, but that in itself does not constitute defeat, just a set back.

There is definitely a need to specifically appropriate the power of the Gospel into precise facets of our life. One general catch all prayer for wholeness is seldom adequate. When we recognise that a particular situation is bringing up feelings of insecurity, or we know we are responding wrongly, or we feel threatened, more than prayer is required. We need to be able to call forth a strong awareness of who we are in Christ. But we won't be equipped to do that if we won't face up to the fact that this particular issue could possibly be something God wants to deal with in our life.

POINTS TO PONDER

(Personally)

1. Jesus promised trouble, but he didn't even imply that we should *be troubled.*

2. Some of our troubles are self-inflicted wounds, which are the direct result of *letting* ourselves be troubled.

3. We are all a long way from an optimal self-image because we are all a long way from an optimal relationship with God.

4. There is quite a catalogue of compensating behaviours and long term results of poor self-image, many of which are sin.

5. It is not uncommon for men and women to handle rejection and other hurts quite differently.

6. Self-pity is a major roadblock in trying to recover our sense of worth, because it retains resentment and foments bitterness.

7. Forgiveness can be completely undone by simply picking up the offence through self-pity.

8. Forgiveness is a decision to release the offender. It costs us our right to get even, but retaining that right is even more costly.

1. The chapter title was pinched from a sermon title by Don Gee of Cambridge-shire
2. John 14:1   **3**. John 16:33   **4**. Proverbs 30:33   **5**. Isaiah 53:6
6. Romans 3:11
7. Low Self-Esteem - Untangling the Roots, Page 37, Carer and Counsellor, Volume 3 Number 2, (Published by CWR)
8. Dr Richard Ecker, The Stress Myth, (Lyon) Appendix A, *Ecker's Laws*, number 8
9. Romans 6:6

Chapter 12

IS YOUR LADDER AGAINST THE RIGHT WALL?

Not too long ago I read a book on personal management by Dr. Steven R. Covey[1] where he introduced the illustration I used in chapter three, of climbing the ladder of success only to find the ladder was against the wrong wall. To me that says it all! One picture is worth 1,000 words, but there are occasions where a very few words can conjure up powerful mental imagery that says even more. Therefore, I want to conclude with a reminder that so much human effort is absolutely wasted, simply because so few of us have any specific goals in life.

Most of us want to be a success but few of us bother to define it. We are working hard at climbing one rung at a time hoping that God or the Tooth Fairy will reward our efforts by clamping our ladder to a star. Christians don't seem to be any better than the rest, possibly even worse. The reason we are probably worse is that we haven't quite worked out how the free will of man works out with the sovereignty of God. We think God is supposed to do all the goal-setting. 'And anyway goals aren't very spiritual. I've been praying about a new car, a rise in pay and enough to re-do the kitchen, but God doesn't seem too interested. I guess I'm too materialistic.'

The fact is, if I think I need a new car I have to save for it. That's a goal and a fairly practical one at that. However necessary this type of goal may be, it has nothing to do with the subject of this book. I am not concerned here with material goals. But I never cease to be amazed at how few Christians seem to set any <u>non-material goals</u>. Christians, above all people, should have plenty of non-material goals. God certainly has an objective for our life - to be conformed to the likeness of his Son.

God's goal for every believer: 'For those God fore-knew he also predestined to be conformed to the likeness of his Son, that he might be the firstborn among many brothers' (Romans 8:29).

God's objective for every believer is to develop the character of Christ. So we know where the heart of God

149

is in this matter. Going back to how the free will of man works out with the sovereignty of God, it is generally agreed that God is a gentleman and seldom forces his will on us. If I want to be conformed to the likeness of Jesus I have to make it my goal as well; the responsibility doesn't all rest with God.

GOALS

We may have goals for what we want to earn and things we want to achieve, but do we have goals for what we want to be? That's what Christianity is all about. We encourage young people to set goals regarding education and career qualifications, which is fairly long range planning and is to be commended. But, once these are achieved, it all seems to fizzle out when it comes to planning. It seems that those who have aimed the highest are the most likely to abandon goal-setting once the original goals are achieved. The chap working up the corporate structure is at least studying what it takes to reach the next rung, but many professionals (of the self-employed type such as doctors and dentists) are completely goalless. They have arrived.

And that's the problem. We are really only concerned with our comfort, and once that is reasonably assured we coast along in what we consider a well-deserved rest for the next forty years. We act as if professional qualifications were the meaning and purpose of life. I recently consulted with a Christian professional who had attempted suicide twice, mainly due to a lack of serious non-material goals. Those who haven't 'arrived' are often too caught up on the treadmill to consider where their life is heading.

We often ask children what they want to be when they grow up. Maybe we need to ask that of ourselves, or better still we need to ask if we want to grow up. After all it is an ongoing process. Christianity is not so much about attaining or achieving as about being. Stephen Covey suggests that those who want to manage their lives prepare a mission statement. I suggest making a Be list. It's not quite the same, but he was writing to a secular audience and I'm more concerned with what I want to be than anything else. My list begins: 'To be God's man, pleasing him by:' and then listing the qualities that I believe he is concerned with in my life, which are characteristics of the kind of person I want to be. I have printed this list (of 13 qualities) on a sheet of paper that fits in my breast pocket notebook so that it is convenient to ponder at idle moments, like traffic jams or long lines at the bank and it frequently features in my quiet time.

I would gladly have included the entire list, even though it would give a fair indication of the areas in my life that are still under construction. The problem is, many would copy it without really thinking through the kind of person they believe *they* need to be to please God. I will tell you this, I got a lot of help from the fruit of the Spirit in Galatians 5:22-23. But the words you use to emphasize

151

the qualities you believe God is most concerned with in *your* life may not be the ones on my list. Before I end this chapter I will provide some other items that may well contribute to your list.

Since this is not a murder mystery, the fact that you are reading the last chapter means there is a better-than-average chance that you have read the entire book. This means you want to do something about your own self-image or help a friend. (Or you got stuck somewhere with no other reading material!) I say this because we have been discussing the propensity to have our ladder against the wrong wall and you may be asking, 'With all the thousands of people believing they are worthless and others totally depressed, what are the odds in favour of real change?'

The odds are excellent. I didn't tell you about my childhood in the introduction to gain sympathy. I did it because I believe there is a law that says people aren't interested in hearing your answer until they are convinced you understand the problem. Well, I do understand because I have been there. When my co-ordination did arrive in time to feature in High School football I became quite difficult to live with. I really can't bear to remember what a show-off I was when I finally found something at which I could excel. And I went through an awful lot of other probing into the mysteries of life, trying to find what it was all about. Coming to Christ made a difference, but not immediately. It took two more decades to discover the distinction between own-ing Christ as Saviour and making him Lord of my life. But when someone who specialized in 'retarded' Christians finally did get through to me I realized my search for reality had ended.

My identity which had been based on achievement suddenly switched to attachment, as illustrated in Jesus' statement:

> I am the vine; you are the branches. If a man remains in me and I in him, he will bear much fruit; apart from me you can do nothing. [2]

I could handle that limitation because I knew I was in good company. I had already come to grips with the fact that Jesus could do nothing without the Father. But even better were the scores of promises of such complete membership in the family of God that God would actually work through my humanity.

GARBAGE IN - GARBAGE OUT

It is possible to be miles ahead in Christian commitment without actually coming to grips with the crucial Christian elements of a healthy self-image. Our mind is enough like a computer that, if computers had been around in Jesus' day, they would have been a favourite illustration. He would have agreed with the axiom 'garbage in - garbage out'. He is aware of the fact that we have all had some very bad programming. The following diagram illustrates the way our self-image is reinforced.

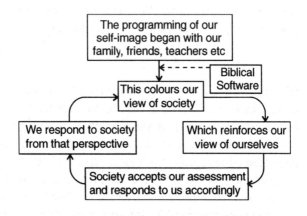

Figure 5 Biblical Software [3]

Our minds are programmed by the significant people in our lives, many of whom had the very best of intentions. If the programming is good, I view and respond to the rest of society as equals. They reciprocate and this reinforces my opinion of myself and society. If the programming is poor I tend to respond to life from that perspective. I walk into a room full of people who obviously have got it together and I keep over to the corner of the room hoping no-one will find out that I have not got it together. They see me acting like a nerd and say 'Gee that guy is acting like a nerd'. I get the idea that they think I'm a nerd so my opinion is reinforced.

154

There are two things to remember about this chart. First, the others haven't got it together and secondly, the software is faulty. The block at the right of the diagram indicates that it is possible to develop some biblical software and so we must. We must have something to play when the adversary starts playing the old programming.

Biblical software is nothing more than Scriptural authority indexed for easy access to our self-talk. The following is my idea of a starting point. You, if you take this seriously, will undoubtedly find many others to add and some which speak much more effectively than the verses I have chosen. These are printed here in the format of a Scripture memory card and we have obtained permission from The International Bible Society for you to photocopy these NIV texts for your own personal use.

I am a new creation
2 Corinthians 5:17 Therefore if anyone is in Christ, he is a new creation; the old has gone, the new has come.

I take my identity from my new nature
Romans 7:20 Now if I do what I do not want to do, it is no longer I who do it, but it is sin living in me that does it.

God loves me
I John 3:1 How great is the love the Father has lavished on us, that we should be called the children of God! And that is what we are!

I have significance in Christ
Ephesians 2:10 We are God's workmanship, created in Christ Jesus to do good works, which God prepares in advance for us to do.

2 Corinthians 5:18 All this is from God, who reconciled us to himself through Christ and gave us the ministry of reconciliation.

I am a significant part of the body of Christ
I Corinthians 12:20-21 There are many parts but one body. The eye cannot say to the hand, "I don't need you!" And the head cannot say to the feet, "I don't need you!"

I must not compare and compete with others who may well be equipped for other functions
2 Corinthians 10:12 We do not dare to classify or compare ourselves with some who commend themselves. When they measure themselves by themselves and compare themselves with themselves, they are not wise.

God will enable me to do those things he calls me to do
I Thessalonians 5:24 Faithful is he that calls you, who also will do it.

I Peter 5:5 God opposes the proud but he enables the humble.
(A Dave Ames paraphrase)

156

Before I conclude, let me say another word or two about making up a Be list. One good source of material, as I have already suggested, is Galatians 5:22 and 23.

> But the fruit of the Spirit is love, joy, peace, patience, kindness, goodness, faithfulness, gentleness and self-control. Against such things there is no law.

SAMPLE BE-LIST (Might begin with) I want to be God's man or woman, pleasing him by:

> Loving others through acceptance and investing in their well-being.

> Being as good, kind, joyful and faithful a friend as circumstances will allow. (That lumps a bit of the fruit together.)

> Being a peacemaker, never criticizing or gossiping about those not present.

I personally I find it hard to resist making a joke, which can sometimes be offensive to others. So I have on my list,

> Having a sense of humour, but not at the expense of others.

Perhaps the following Start and Stop list will provide a few more ideas for your Be list.

Stop:

>Comparing myself with others
>Identifying with my old nature
>Going on feelings
>Negative self-talk
>Allowing myself to indulge in self-centredness

Start:

>Obeying God
>Accepting responsibility for who I am, and what I am to become
>Renewing my mind
>Investing in others
>Expecting God to use me
>Relying on God, as an acknowledgement that he is committed to working through my humanity at any time I become available.

I hope these lists prove to be effective tools in building a rightly based self-image, and developing an attitude of humble confidence.

POINTS TO PONDER

(While you are working on your Be list)

1. Most of us want to be a success but few of us have defined it.

2. If I want to be conformed to the likeness of Jesus I have to make it my goal as well; the responsibility doesn't all rest with God.

3. Few Christians set any non-material goals, when Christians above all people should have goals for what they want to become.

4. Our minds, like computers, have been programmed by the significant others in our lives, but the programming is faulty and we need to develop some biblical software.

5. Biblical software consists mainly of scriptural authority easily indexed for easy access to our self-talk.

1. The 7 Habits of Highly Effective People Stephen R. Covey, Simon & Schuster, New York
2. John 15:5
3. An adaptation of an illustration from Living With Your Emotions, Norman Wright (Harvest House 1979) Page 9.

Looking Up the Aisle?

**'The book that launched
a thousand marriages'**
(several times over).

Marriage Preparation need not be done in a classroom
situation. Nor does it have to be a burden for the pastor.
Looking Up the Aisle? affords an efficient, practical
and inexpensive vehicle to provide couples with exactly
what they need at this crucial juncture.

Looking Up the Aisle? is a user friendly workbook
providing a biblical perspective on various facets of
marriage. Chapters followed by questions to be an-
swered by each partner separately, provide a suitable
catalyst for dialogue helping couples explore their expectations, similarities and harness their diversities.

According to the authors, Dave and Joyce Ames, 'Christian marriage preparation consists mainly of identifying
expectations and forming realistic ones into goals that
reflect Christian values'. *Looking Up the Aisle?* is
available in Christian shops.

For those interested in helping couples prepare for
marriage, there is also a kit available containing 200
minutes of seminar talks by the authors, twelve pages of
preprinted notes x2, and a copy of *Looking Up the
Aisle?* Contact *MISSION TO MARRIAGE* to order kit.